THINK CRICKET

COMPETE MENTALLY

WRITTEN BY
Christopher Bazalgette
& John Appleyard

FOREWORD BY
John Barclay
MCC President 2010

G2 entertainment

First published in the UK in 2011

www.G2ent.co.uk

Printed and bound printed in the EU

ISBN 978-1-907803-24-6

Contents

Foreword

Nobody has given more thought to THINK – Cricket than the indefatigable Chris Bazalgette. But he is of course more than just a great thinker; he is also a great doer who sets an example to those who love the game. This lovely and important volume is crammed full of his experiences from a career that has graced the world of club cricket for more decades than I care to remember. It is perceptive and understanding.

Chris and John know that cricket is a hard game in which there are a multitude of twists and turns, and yet in this book they have produced a mini-bible into which players of all ages and abilities can dip, in the secure knowledge that their skills will thereby improve. It is a straightforward book too, where there is something for everybody: batting, bowling and fielding tips, and a few words on captaincy, umpiring and scoring as well. This is definitely a book to be slipped into the cricket bag as an essential piece of equipment, alongside bat, pads, gloves and box. We all like to have something in life on which to hang our hats and these pages should do the trick for most of us.

Many people reveal their secrets of success grudgingly, but not so with Chris and John. They have written a book here that is bang up to date, but yet never fails to appreciate the experience taught by history and times past. Gamesmanship plays no part in their scheme of things and the game for them is infinitely more important than the individual.

This book is full of advice which will improve your game and, who knows, might work wonders for your technique and also do much for your morale. There is always so much to learn about cricket and so much to investigate. Read this book and you'll improve.

J. R. T. Barclay

Director of Cricket and Coaching, Arundel Castle Cricket Foundation.

MCC President 2010

Manager, England Tour of Zimbabwe and New Zealand 1996-97

Assistant Manager, England Tour of South Africa and the World Cup in India 1995-96. Captain of Sussex 1981-1986

Preface

The majesty of the game of cricket is that it is not just a physical activity. It is not simply a matter of how strong or tough one is, or how fast one can run, but a combination of the mental and physical strengths and abilities needed to outwit your opposition.

THINK – Cricket stresses that there is much more to the game when your mind is fully focused. It aims to open everyone's mind to a wider dimension of the game, and to provide a subtle awareness which should mean better results.

Many cricketers, even those participating every week, do so without realising how their performance can be improved dramatically.

THINK – Cricket is for amateur cricketers who lack the resources to look at videos of those who are going to oppose them, as do professional cricketers, and have no professional coach to remind them of what to look for in each game they play.

However, everything discussed in this book should be equally valuable at whatever level you are playing, but it is the amateur or club cricketer who has the most to gain.

Apart from such cricketers in the Test Match playing countries that are full members of ICC, those in the ever-increasing number of associate and affiliate member countries will benefit from reading this book.

Both authors have been associated with and have played in many of the above-mentioned countries and throughout the world. We have personal experience of the immense enthusiasm to be found. There is plenty of thought-provoking advice within these chapters.

The Thinker by Rodin located at the Musée Rodin in Paris

Note: Cricket is a game for women and girls as well as men and boys. The use of pronouns indicating the male gender is purely for brevity.

Scope and Organisation

Our content is divided into chapters along the lines of cricket itself: Captaincy, batting, bowling, fielding, wicket-keeping, umpiring and scoring, and psychology. All are presented in detail from the thinking angle.

It will be appreciated how much the Captain has to do and especially if the reader is in the 'hot seat', the importance of leadership will be fully perceived.

Once the reader has found a particular factor works, then the true value of the book will mean so much more. The batting and bowling chapters should be enjoyed particularly, and there the true impact of the mental approach will be absorbed. Increasing the mental input will lead to the realisation that new levels of performance are attainable.

As the most important member of the team is the Captain, first we focus on his thinking process, his responsibilities before and after the match and, of course, his leadership on the field of play.

We emphasise that a batsman should mentally prepare for an innings; he should not just reach the crease and play the ball without thought. He should be reading the bowler, looking around the field for scoring opportunities and asking himself if a tempting gap has been left open as a trap? It is seldom there because there are not enough fielders!

We discuss the mental approach of the fast bowler, his opening spell, his body language and, when rested, his attitude to bowling again later in the innings. Following on we introduce the slow bowler with variations of guile, flight and spin all demanding concentration. The bowler has to learn how to read a batsman, search for his weakness and set a trap that causes him to self-destruct.

Fielding, whether close to the bat or in the outfield demands a lot of thought and concentration. The fielder should be thinking about how he can support the bowler and his team-mates, and he will find he is more in the game, thus considerably enriching this activity.

The wicket-keeper has to concentrate every time the ball is bowled and, besides the physical activity, cannot relax. He must observe and provide a detailed assessment of each batsman for each bowler, and for his Captain whenever asked.

Each match, whether limited overs or a time game requires thought from all the participants. The more 'professional' the team the more scientific will be their approach. Pre-match preparation will include a team talk and a plan for selective attacks on the opposition, both in the field and with the bat. The Captain will explain his strategy, the team will collectively .Absorb this book and realise how much the brain can assist in gaining the best from the game. Every ball requires mental input, apply it and one is able to enjoy cricket so much more.

Overview Of Chapters

THINK – Success

THINK – Success should be the aim for everyone starting his or her life. However, in this context we are thinking of batting and bowling. Taking batting first, if you followed these instructions and achieved each activity well you would eventually become a very good batsman.

Similarly, if you followed the process for bowling you would become a very good bowler.

Even if you were to accomplish the tasks set for both challenges and asked the professionals for their advice and followed it, you should be a good exponent of batting and/or bowling. The only other factor you require is luck.

THINK – Captaincy

The Captain has a wide range of responsibilities to both his team and his club. This chapter is divided into sections describing each area specifically. As a club Captain he has more duties than leading his team during a match. These are all highlighted in this chapter. Even more important is his ability to handle people and his judgement in gaining the best from each player, thus moulding a team together.

THINK – Batting

Although cricket is a team game, batting is each individual's responsibility and each team member should learn not only how to bat but also be able to perform. This chapter will help all batsmen to learn how to improve their performance even before reaching the 'middle', to outwit the bowlers and score runs more easily.

Learn how to build an innings to the benefit of the team and your batting partners.

THINK – Bowling

Good bowling, whether fast, medium or slow, requires a flexible mind. The bowler has to combine with the fielders to outthink the batsman. This chapter reminds the bowler to think before every ball, to study the batsman and work out how to dismiss him. The art of slow bowling will intrigue the reader, especially batsmen who think every slow bowler should be hit to the boundary almost every ball.

THINK – Fielding Positions

A set of diagrams suggesting different field settings for each style of bowling.

THINK – Fielding

There is probably more to be learnt in this chapter than any other. The reader is alerted to how they can support the bowler and help take wickets, even though they are not actually fielding the ball themselves. A good fielding side can destroy the rhythm of good batsmen and the more your team improves in this department of the game, the more everyone will enjoy playing cricket.

THINK – Wicket-keeping

The wicket-keeper is a special player in every fielding side. The whole team performance in the field will revolve around him. The 'keeper's enthusiasm and ability should enhance the ability of the team's bowlers, should provide a spur to all the fielders and supply a continual assessment of the batsman's faults and weaknesses to each bowler and his Captain. This chapter offers wicket-keepers the detail on how to 'read' the game and be an even greater support to his team-mates.

THINK – Learning

For parents, Guardians and teachers: introducing sport to any child will require a gentle and delicate approach.

Especially with cricket, as it is more complicated, it is vital that each session is fun and is a slow progression in the learning process.

THINK – Training

Physical preparation, whether mental or physical or their combinations are vital for successful sportsmen and sportswomen. This will be inherent as the learning process progresses.

Different disciplines within cricket require different forms of training. Amongst the leading authorities there is a certain amount of conjecture, based on encouraging bone and muscle structure to establish shape and form for the best style for a specific youth, but to be extremely care conscious not to risk overuse to risk damage in later years.

Current thinking demands 'warm-ups' and 'warm-downs', the use of ice baths for fast bowlers at the end of play. Within both sessions, it is not necessarily the need to create fast movement but to stretch all the specific muscles to ease them into use.Many earlier trainers believed their subjects should be hardened to be able to perform over long periods and become resistant to injury by more and more play.

THINK – Practice

This is the most important single factor in developing the young sportsperson. Correct clothing and footwear, using the right equipment that is not too heavy and proper protection encourage participation, whereas the lack of protection may scar their enjoyment forever.

The need for organised and planned practice is vital for the serious cricketer. However, the individual can develop various senses using basic exercises. Practice and more practice is always important. You can never practise too much. Do not forget group strategy or the need of fielding.

THINK – Concentration

Every paragraph of this book is aimed at helping you play cricket better, but if you fail to concentrate when it matters then all is lost. Were you to try and concentrate all the time, the effect would be so weakening you would be more likely to fail as well, so this section endeavours to tell you when to concentrate as a fielder, batsman or bowler and wicket-keeper or Captain.

To start with it will be hard and you will not be able to be as effective as you want, however, with practice you will improve. Most of this process is natural and therefore it will not be necessary to worry about it. If you are aware of the important occasions then that will help you not just be a better cricketer but also enable you to be the best cricketer.

THINK – Experience

Every action from our first awareness quickly passes to become our experience. Therefore it is vital to recognise the important events that should be stored, for us to gain from our own and others' experiences. Good experience often begets confidence.

THINK – Discipline

Both the umpire and scorer should be cleared by CRB. Discipline is not about authority, but it is about your personal control in every situation in which you find yourself. It could be described as one's personal pride to perform well. Looking smart and behaving as one should behave. Being a winner and supporting your team-mates is all part of the same programme.

THINK – Psychology

The very word means the study of mental processes and motives; we have only touched on this specialist subject. In a way the entire book is centred around cricket psychology and not a lot needs to be added.

The pressure of winning and losing, at every level the game is played, causes stresses and requires motivation. This chapter offers readers the opportunity to learn the basics of this highly sophisticated subject and prepares them for further study if that is what is desired.

THINK – Umpiring And Scoring

To play cricket you need two umpires, whose job is to impartially interpret the Laws, many of which state that for a person to be 'out' it will be in the umpire's opinion. Cricket does not have **rules**, other than those detailing a certain type of competition.

Umpires communicate with the scorers using various signals to signify either runs scored or batsmen dismissed or just the game unfolding. The umpires also control the attitude of sportsmanship and competitiveness between the teams.

If your team has a club scorer you are very lucky, often the Captain will ask players to act as scorer for a number of overs, so everybody should learn how to score, most of scoring is common sense, concentration and being neat and tidy. You must know how to interpret the signals from the umpire and use the correct symbols when putting these details on the scoresheet. The more information on the scoresheet will make it easier for those wanting to understand what happened in the game in the future.

THINK – Success

For Batsmen Who Wish To Make Runs

The process of becoming a good batsman starts from the basis of learning which balls one must defend and those from which you can score runs. However good a cricketer you are – it is impossible to score runs from every ball. Some you will not need to play, some you will play defensively and some you will attack.

When you start to play cricket you will need to learn the very basics: how to hold the bat, your position before the ball is bowled (stance), the correct shots to play – depending on the type of ball bowled – how good your eyes are at seeing each ball, the relative speed of each ball and at what point you need to hit it; this is called timing.

You will need to build your strength and keep very fit and athletic and practice and practice.

You will need to learn each discipline of the art of bowling, bowling actions, how each bowler delivers the ball, when it is bad bowling or a deceptive ball, the gaps the Captain of the opposition has left and the traps he has set for you.

You need to learn groundsmanship, so that you can understand how the ball will react with the ground when bowled at various speeds, how much deviation is likely when cutters are bowled and similarly how much spin either a finger spinner or wrist spinner will achieve.

Just as important as 'reading the pitch' is the ability to understand the effect of the atmospherics, how much the ball is likely to swing and at what speed it will swing and whether the opposition has any bowler who can gain movement in the air from the current conditions.

You will have to ascertain from the field set by the bowler how accurate the bowler is likely to be, and the confidence the Captain has for his bowler. Who the good fielders are, who are left or right-handed throwers, where the dangers are – not only for yourself but also for your partner.

As your experience grows you will need to know how to recognise body language and how your performance, your confidence, and the way you react to each situation, affects the opposition.

Now add the relationship you have with the batsmen of your own side and how you inter relate with each of them. It will also help to know their abilities, their aspirations, the signals they give out, plus their strengths and weaknesses.

Other factors that should be included in the equation are everybody's current form, previous form against each opposition, the situation of the game and the instructions given by your own Captain.

There are two more very important studies you will have to have conquered before you are the complete batsman, the first is to read each 'bowler's hand' as he delivers the ball and the other one is the choice of shot you make whilst the ball is being propelled towards you. Some of these areas can be learned in the nets, others you will have to learn playing in a match. With determination and dedication, practice, training and talking to those who know; you will gain in confidence, scoring runs for yourself will create memories, which develops more confidence and later experience.

Most important of all is that the batsman's set up is vital, playing straight, concentration, patience and balance.

Batting is simple and as long as the batsman understands what he is trying to achieve during his innings he will be well placed to succeed.

Batting is as much about mental strength and concentration as it is about physical ability, it only takes a second's loss of concentration to end your innings. Play within the limits of your ability. Do not play shots that you haven't mastered!!!! All are vital for the quality batsman who wants to score runs.

For Bowlers Who Want To Take Wickets

The art of bowling, taking wickets, also includes denying the batsman from scoring runs, but in most cases he cannot score runs if he has been dismissed.

The first requirement is to be able to bowl accurately and this is called bowling 'Line and Length'. It does not matter whether you are going to be a fast bowler, medium pace or slow bowler who uses spin to outwit the batsman, 'Line and Length' are always two factors you must achieve.

These two needs are never believed by the young cricketer, as whoever reads these words will also fail to believe it. It still remains a fact. The sooner you can understand, believe and master 'Line & Length' then you will start to learn how to bowl well.

You must know how to bat otherwise it will be impossible to understand the batsman's weaknesses. You need to be able to quickly assess how to 'read' the batsman, his ability, his body language, his amount of concentration, how good he is and whether he is able to read your bowling.

Obviously the state of the game will feature strongly on how he will attempt to score and his confidence from the start of his innings. Besides your ability at containing his stroke play, you have the wicket-keeper and nine fielders helping you; they, together with your Captain, should help to detract from his success.

Once you have learnt that you can bowl the ball where you wish, you should learn to bowl at different speeds, that achieved, you can develop whether you are going to depend on speed, moving the ball by 'swing' or cutting it off the seam. Alternatively, you will bowl using spin as your deception.

Like each batsman, you will need to know about groundsmanship, and atmospherics, gamesmanship, sowing the seed of doubt in the batsman's mind. Learn to offer him the ball he can hit and then make it harder and harder till he becomes over confident and tries to hit the ball which is not just possible and loses his wicket. This is unlikely if you cannot bowl accurately.

Two factors that are not often considered are the height of the batsman and your own height, because the trajectory of the ball is another very key factor that is not considered.

As you grow older, your action will change, often without you realising. It is important to ensure you keep your fundamental action similar, that of being 'side-on' when you deliver the ball, pivoting over the front knee, keeping your arm close to your ear in the perpendicular at the point of delivery – there are exceptions to this shape for the left arm spinner, the right arm leg/googly spin bowler and the in-swing bowler, but you should gain the help of a professional when learning and developing these styles.

Whenever you deliver the ball you should be concentrating on where you wish to pitch the ball.

Although you and your Captain decide where your fielders are to be placed, keep a check on their positions as ALL fielders wander. Just five yards out of place can ruin your plan, and once you have induced a false stroke it might mean several overs bowled before you can strike again.

Do not be afraid of moving your fielders, if the batsman is any good it might mean he will mentally wonder why you have made the change and again you are putting another doubt into his mind. It also gives you more opportunities.

Like the best Captains who must often risk defeat, if they are to win; a slow bowler must sometimes allow his bowling to be hit to induce the batsman to lose his wicket.

If you have a good Captain and a good wicket-keeper they should advise you about each batsman's ability and weaknesses, but be careful to recognise the difference between learning about the batsman and the other side of the coin, which is when your wicket-keeper or other fielders repeatedly tell you how to bowl. You must have confidence in your own ability.

Always remember all batsmen are greedy.

If you are a slow bowler they will consider they can hit you out of the park at will; you do not need to encourage them.

Sadly, many captains are only interested in the batsmen not making any runs, tending to insist the slow spin bowler bowls 'flat' and too fast, this minimises effect as the ball has not time to grip the pitch, subtle variations are lost and the art of flight and guile are diminished.

Actually a good spinner or slow bowler can be 'worth his weight in gold' and provide his side with *'a perfect antidote to the medium pace trundler'*.

Ask any hard-hitting batsman which he would rather face – he will almost always say that he likes the ball coming onto him.

What is a good length?

From an academic point of view it is a point about three feet in front of the batsman when he plays forward in a defence position. But in a match situation it is very different. Each batsman will have a different spot, it will depend on your pace at which you bowl, whether he is playing in a defence or attacking mode, the trajectory of the ball and the height and reach of the batsman, coupled with the range of shots he is likely to play.

As a golden rule no slow bowler should ever bowl short. Unless you bowl very fast and you have knowledge that the batsman cannot play short bowling it should not be necessary to bowl short.

THINK – Captaincy

Gladiators!

This section is intended to give the reader a variety of factors that may not be found in any coaching manuals. Some of the points discussed will be of a general nature but the 'thinking' approach is the angle from which we discuss this vital subject.

To simplify this process we have sub-divided the various duties of the Captain and applied this thinking approach to each area of responsibility.

Captaincy Within The Club Structure

The Club Captain should automatically be a member of the Club's committee, and will probably report to the Club Chairman. His responsibilities are numerous and involve selection, training and coaching, and player discipline, as well as maintaining an image which is respected, particularly by the younger members. His body language on and off the field will always convey a message, so that he should enthuse confidence and ability at all times.

His personality will be one reason why his fellow players elected him in the first place. He must therefore always set a good example, and be communicative and efficient. Dealing with players requires knowing them as individuals and then being positive, yet good humoured so as not to undermine their confidence.

Developing his squad of players means letting them all know his plans. Debating attainable targets, and discussing with each individual methods of training and practice, will ensure the goal is achieved.

From time to time the Captain should arrange team meetings to talk tactics and, if possible, watch coaching videos.

Targets will not always be reached. The Captain must not become angry or frustrated, as this mood will discourage progress. No one likes to fail, and provided a player makes an effort, he should be praised and encouraged. Being Captain of a club, or of any team, is an honour. It is a big job and when it works well, is a very rewarding activity.

Captaincy Before The Match

Every Captain whether playing at home or away should talk with the groundsman. It does not matter how much he thinks he knows about pitches, he should always try and discuss the state of the pitch and how the groundsman thinks it is going to play.

It is of greater importance if the groundsman is your own 'Club Man', and he should be made to feel important in his role within the Club. In most cases the Captain will learn vital factors to help his decisions throughout the game, and when playing away it is just as important to consult the man who has done the work on the pitch.

The Captain has the responsibility to ensure his team knows how to find the opposition ground and how they intend to travel. If playing at home, he will need to check that the secretary has informed the opposition how to find his ground. When playing at home his other duties include arranging meals and helpers, checking that umpires and scorers have been organised and ensuring that everybody knows the hours of play. He should also check that the opposition dressing room is clean and all the facilities are in working order, and be ready to welcome the opposition, so that the match starts off in the right spirit. Good manners are not a sign of weakness.

Once the Captain has discussed the pitch conditions with the groundsman, he then 'goes out to toss up'. What does he decide to do if he wins the toss? Ninety-nine times out of every hundred he should BAT. This will be a learning curve, for it is very hard to put into writing the case for asking the opposition to bat first, unless your own batting is very weak or, alternatively your bowling is weak and you have a very strong batting team. However, your groundsman may suggest otherwise if a difficult pitch is likely to improve during a game.

Team Selection

In most clubs the Captain is the person to have the final choice in the selection of the team. Much will depend on the qualities of the players he has at his disposal, but in basic terms, he should look for a good wicket- keeper, as in the field the team hinges around this position.

He will need at least five good batsmen, two fast bowlers, a spinner or slow bowler plus one or two all-rounders. Try and blend maturity with inexperience, flair with solidity. The job of the Captain is to mould them to perform as a team, to help each other and support each other. To succeed he must understand their individuality, but encourage them to be positive and successful. It is vital to bring each of them into the game, so they can see they have contributed to the whole team's achievement.

The Captain must remember his first responsibility is to try and win the game.

The Captain's Pre-Match Planning

Before the match he should decide on his batting order. He should work out who is going to do the bowling and be aware of the strengths and weaknesses in the field – who throws right-handed and left-handed, the runners and non-runners, those who will field close-in and those who prefer to field further away from the bat, as well as those who can throw from the boundary. He must also work out that, having set a certain field for one opening bowler, what happens at the end of the over when the other man is bowling. Will the key fielders be in the correct positions? For instance, it is always good, with a right-handed batsman, to have a left-handed thrower at cover point, as the ball will tend to curve from the bat to his left side. Pre-planning does not mean a Captain should only have one plan and stick rigidly to it. He obviously starts with a basic plan, but must adapt to the circumstances as the game evolves, reacting to change quietly and unobtrusively, but effectively. When 'setting' the field he should do it with confidence.

Leadership During The Match – Batting

Every batsman is nervous before he goes out to bat, some more than others, for we **all** want to achieve. Even when making out the batting order, the Captain can inadvertently undermine the confidence of a batsman.

Obviously not everyone can be batting 'up the order'. Instead of stating someone cannot bat well, the Captain should **be positive**. He may either explain they are going 'to have a bowl', or discuss that one member might be able to score faster, or that at a specific stage in the innings, it might require a more steadying influence.

Let batsmen know your plan of campaign, how many runs you want them to score and how long you intend the team to bat. Any pressures you can remove from them will improve their chances. Remind them of their strengths, if you know anything about the bowlers then tell your batsmen.

Discuss the positions in which the opposition Captain has placed his fielders. Point out the weaknesses. When a batsman is out allow him to unwind, and then perhaps discuss the opposition's bowling, so that other members of the side can benefit. If dealing with a young player, it may be a good idea to suggest that he write out what he thought of his performance (for himself): the pluses and the minuses, how he could have improved his innings and what he should practise before he next goes out to bat. As wickets fall, keep your later batsmen advised as to what you want from each of them. Ensure that everyone knows the position in the order that they are batting, before **you** go out to bat.

Leadership In The Field

The job of the Captain when his side is fielding is even more important. **He must insist that all the fielders watch him at some moment after every ball is bowled.** Should he wish to make an adjustment to the fielder's position, it helps if the batsman is not aware of the change.

Watch the Captain!

Except in junior cricket, the bowler should know what fielding positions he requires for his type of bowling. He knows what he wants to bowl and so together he and the Captain set the field.

The Captain should advise the bowler whether he wants to attack, or keep runs to a minimum by being on the defensive, or both, if possible.

It is important for the Captain to place himself in a position where he can observe the batsman, can speak with the bowler without too much disruption of the game, and can be close to most of the fielders during actual play. The Captain should communicate with the wicket-keeper at regular intervals, because he is in the best position to assess how well the bowler is bowling.

During play, if the bowler is not bowling well, or if a batsman is scoring more runs than is expected, it is for the Captain to suggest a change in the bowler's 'field' (fielding positions). Do this quietly in consultation with your bowler, for if you make it too obvious it can undermine the bowler's confidence and help the batsman.

Both the Captain and the bowler will need to make small adjustments for each batsman. It is very important for every Captain to know what his bowler is trying to do; similarly it is important for the bowler to tell him.

When setting a field the gaps are probably more important than where fielders are placed, for a gap may lure the batsman into making a false shot and possibly losing his wicket.

If your bowlers fail to break through, try changing key fielders to another fielding position. Some batsmen will not notice you making the change.

It is vital the Captain communicates with his team, specifically encouraging and talking with his players. For example: one of your players may be purely a batsman but also a good boundary fielder, and therefore away from his team-mates. He might feel left out of the game, so give him an opportunity to feel part of it. Bring him closer in for a few overs, probably exchanging him for another fielder. If a fielder becomes bored he loses concentration.

If you think a fielder is not happy with the position you have put him in, ask him if he wants to move. Alternatively, if he is a specialist in speed of movement or catching, then tell him how important it is for **him** to be fielding in that position.

A good Captain encourages and congratulates his players. It may happen that you have an older man fielding in a position where he is unable to be as quick as you wish him to be and he misses the ball you thought he could stop. Remember you put him there in the first place. Do not move him immediately, leave it to the next over. It may help him keep his confidence and try harder. If possible plan to put a younger man close to him to cover the running activity.

The Captain should also let his whole team know his policy on appealing and what their attitude should be when decisions go against them, because if there is no plan it is likely to be the moment when concentration lapses and a proper chance is missed.

The Captain must be forever on his guard to make sure that fielders do not wander out of position, because runs and wickets can be lost by a single lapse of concentration. This should be checked before the bowler begins his run-up at the start of each over. It is also in the bowler's interest to make a regular check.

One of the most important parts of captaincy is choosing which bowlers to bowl, when they should bowl and which bowlers could bowl together. A Captain's thinking should revolve around which bowlers have the most ability within the team. There are traditions concerning who starts, when changes are required and which type of bowlers should replace the earlier ones.

Usually fast bowlers open the bowling, as they require the hard new ball to gain swing and bounce. However this is not the only option, for your opposing opening batsmen normally face the fast bowlers, and it may unsettle them if you start with a slow bowler. Fast bowlers aim to achieve an early breakthrough, though sometimes the batsmen give the appearance they are struggling, yet a wicket fails to fall. The Captain has to weigh up the key moment when he must change his bowlers, and perhaps in this case the bowlers are simply playing the batsmen in. At this point the Captain might have another medium to medium-fast bowler and the natural tendency would be to introduce him at this point.

But it is much more effective to bring on a slower bowler, even for a few overs, as then the batsman must assess a very different pace and bounce. Every time the bowling changes all the factors have to go through his mind. Some batsmen take longer than others to re-adjust. The Captain must attempt to stop the batsman getting 'set'.

When a Captain is handling his 'fast' bowlers, he must be aware that they tire more quickly than the other bowlers, so that to be effective they must bowl in short spells. When a wicket falls, the Captain might decide to bring his fast bowler back at the opposite end to the one who took the wicket. He should be also aware that bowlers can sometimes bowl better when they bowl in pairs.

In any case to keep pressure on the batsman he must manipulate his bowlers and the fielders to squeeze hard enough to create the fall of a wicket.

The Captain who frequently changes his bowling may be the more successful, but if someone is bowling well don't change him just for the sake of it.

A problem that often arises is the situation where you have batted first and not scored many runs. When the opposition bat, your opening bowlers keep their batsmen under control, but do not actually beat the bat.

The natural attitude is to keep such bowlers on with the thought you will build pressure on the batsmen to score faster, **actually what you are doing is to play the batsmen in and because they do not need many runs they will later naturally score faster anyway.** If you have slow bowlers who you would normally bowl, you, **MUST put them on early,** otherwise should they fail, you will be unable to recover your position. Change of pace and angle/style are also vital commodities, you must keep the batsman on the edge – he will know that your team found it hard to score runs and therefore every pressure you can add to the situation is vital. But wickets are paramount and their taking should concentrate your endeavour.

Captaincy After The Match

Whatever the result of the match, the Captain's duties are still not finished. He will be responsible for the collection of match fees, unless he has delegated the job to another member of the team, which is a good idea in that other team members become used to taking on responsibilities. He must be ready to entertain the opposition Captain, ensure the bar is properly manned, look after the umpires and scorers and ensure the scoresheet has been properly completed. He must advise his opponents of their match dues and collect them.

When playing at home, he should have asked his groundsman if he wants the covers put on a specific 'strip' for the next match.

If the Club flag was put up then this must be taken down. The sight screens may need to be moved; all such duties have to be remembered. If players are doing bar duties, the Captain must make sure that everybody takes their turn, and the players should be encouraged to entertain their opponents after the match, whatever the result.

It is a good idea for the Captain to make his own report of the match, keeping the season's reports in a file, so he can assess any theme of success or failure (and even make notes of how his decisions influenced the result!)

He can record his observations on each of his players and encourage his vice Captain to do the same and compare notes.

If time allows the Captain should have a team discussion on the points that arise and discuss how they all might improve. However care must be taken **not** to over criticise, as stated previously **be positive** not **negative**.

Recognise good points which may be stored in their memories. It may be the Captain's responsibility after the match to prepare a write-up for the local press, although he could delegate this task to another player.

The Captain's Job

Besides the administrative activity off the field, he must be a positive person. There are so many occasions in conversation with club members at all levels where he needs to be on his guard against undermining confidence.

This factor is especially important when dealing with the youth of the club, likely to be even more vulnerable than the more hardened campaigners. Everyone needs encouragement especially when they are 'going through a bad patch'.

Morale

In the field the Captain contributes far more by his body language than by shouting and clapping his hands and gesticulating.

The Captain of the Club is a real job, with great responsibilities, and when it all 'comes right' it is a very rewarding activity. It is a great honour, yet should not be undertaken unless a player is prepared to make a full commitment to the task.

If you are the Captain of a team **within** the Club you have the opportunity to learn the job. You only have the responsibility for your team, yet you should be just as dedicated in carrying out your tasks and looking after the welfare of your team-mates. You need to learn to communicate with the Club Captain and more senior club officials, as well as with the teams below your standard.

Keep your head down.

THINK – Batting

The development of batting technique will depend on each individual's experiences from an early age. Much will depend on the influences of those who trained the individual, so it is very important to obtain the advice of a professional coach early in the learning curve.

For whilst guiding the youth in the styles of batting, both in attack and defence, the key is to allow natural flair to blossom, thus encouraging confidence, which leads to the ability to hit the ball.

Similarly, to fill a young head with too many thoughts and technical detail, will bore the most enthusiastic beginner.

Hence **THINK – Batting** assumes that a player already has some batting skills and wants to improve his game.

Some vital knowledge for batsmen:

- Good sight
- Hand and eye co-ordination
- Timing
- Concentration
- Patience
- Fitness
- Understanding bowling actions
- Determination

Before Going Out To Bat

Every batsman has to prepare himself mentally before going to the crease. Most cricketers have some sort of nerves, because none of us wish to fail; however, this state helps us to concentrate better and if harnessed properly brings us to a point of 'readiness'.

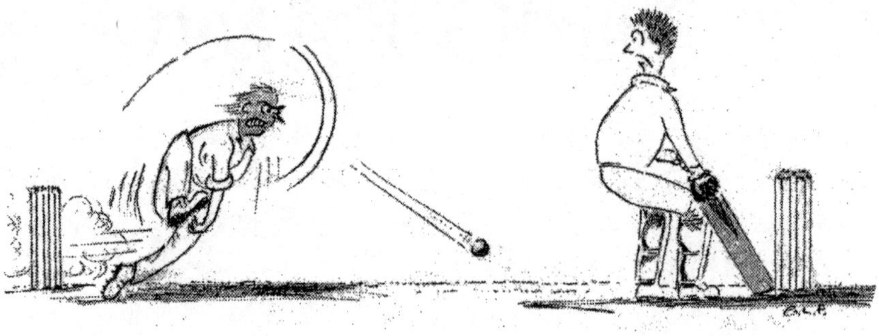

I've just remembered what I forgot to put on!

Ensure you have accustomed yourself to the light and if you are not an opening batsman, you should have observed the fielding positions and found out what the bowler is trying to bowl before arriving at the crease. It is important to notice which fielders throw with their left or right hand, who are nimble, or are the quickest runners.

Other factors include whether a fielder can throw-in directly from the boundary or alternatively does he struggle to throw a long way. Note those who are moving well before the bowler delivers the ball and those who only amble a few paces. Make a note of the gaps in the field and ask yourself why the gaps have been left.

Check whether a bowler changes his pace (bowls a slower or faster ball) or changes his action. Can you see any signal between the bowler and the wicket-keeper? Does the bowler use the width of the crease? Take note how much bounce the bowler is gaining from the pitch and whether it is the same at both ends.

Consider with whom you are likely to be batting and discuss your running between the wickets. Think about using 'soft hands' to hit the ball slowly towards the covers or on the leg side to steal a run. When you are preparing your innings remember the good shots you have played in past innings, because this will give you confidence. Ascertain from the Captain what his 'game-plan' is and how you fit into the plan.

When You Reach The Crease

Initially you will only be able to concentrate on staying in, so it is a good idea to set yourself targets, such as batting for the first over, then say 15 minutes, then an hour and so on. Endeavour to rotate the strike, so the bowler has to continually react to the change of batsman, which is particularly helpful if one of you is left-handed. If a fast bowler is bowling a good length and the 'keeper is standing back it is sometimes a good idea to take your guard two or three feet down the pitch. This is often very upsetting to the bowler as he may not realise why you are driving him off the front foot. It will also tend to make him bowl shorter, so that you deny him the opportunity to swing the ball. If he hits your pads in this situation you are less likely to be given out LBW. Anything you can do to upset his rhythm will improve your chances of success. As your innings progresses and you start timing the ball better, plan your shots. For instance, by playing fractionally earlier or later you may be able to play to the left or right of specific fielders. Always play to your strengths. Attack where you know you can score runs, defend in the areas where you are not so strong.

As your innings becomes easier work out how to outwit the bowler. Talk with your partner and find out whether he is equally happy facing both bowlers. Maybe you each prefer different bowlers. By planning quick singles you can arrange to play the bowler you prefer.

When your partner is out, you must look after the new batsman, helping to maintain the scoring rate while the new batsman settles down.

Opening Batsmen

The job of each opener is primarily to stay in and establish a start to the team's innings, and to see the opening bowlers 'off'. They have to learn about the fielding side as they commence their innings, being careful to notice the playing characteristics of each fielder and reacting accordingly. The longer they are at the crease the better it is for their

Keep your mind focused on the ball.

team-mates, who may learn and build on the start that the opening batsmen have given the side. It is probably of greater importance than at any other time that the 'strike' is rotated. Look for the singles.

As an opener there is extra pressure on you when you are chasing a target, or if the match is based on a limited number of overs. If that is the case you have to balance the need to wear the bowlers down against the need to keep the run rate going. If you become too 'bogged down' you may have to consider hitting out, even at the risk of ending your innings, to make way for someone who can score quicker. This will be determined by the quality of those following you in the batting order, for by this time you will have 'got your eye in', while the new batsman will take a period of time to reach that stage.

Middle Order Batsmen

As a middle order batsman you should be a more forceful player, and as such be able to build on the base your openers have set up.

Your thinking process will have taken place as we have already described, so your first target is to become fully acclimatised to the conditions. As soon as you find you are timing the ball properly you can accelerate the run rate. While you are 'getting set' you will still need to 'rotate the strike'. If successful, no doubt the opposition will endeavour to unsettle you by changing the bowler. You become the person in control, for the new bowler has to settle into his rhythm, during which time you should be able to take command. Whoever comes out on top will be determined to show whose confidence is the greater.

Vital Knowledge For All Batsmen

Many batsmen decide they will specialise in being aggressive, taking command and ignoring the bowler's technique. This is foolish, because if they are unaware of what the bowler is trying to do they can only depend on their eyesight and their reactions once the ball has pitched.

However, if the batsman is able to recognise a bowling action and watch both the bowler's arm and hand, he will have vital fractions of seconds to adjust his stroke. The more he knows about the bowler's technique the more he will understand, particularly with a slow bowler, how a batsman can be lured into a trap. Only then can he ensure he avoids it.

Especially For The Young

When you are a young player and you have completed your innings, it is a good idea to write out a description of how you batted. Describe your good shots and the bad ones, make specific notes on what was wrong. Learn from a better player how to put things right and what you must practise before you next play a match. How did your play fit into your Captain's game plan?

Could you have improved on it? Look at all aspects and make a note on what you think you learnt from the innings.

How To Read The Bowler

On arrival at the crease take a real look at where the fielders and wicket-keeper are standing, which should give you an idea as to the speed of the bowler. The set of the field should tell you which way he is hoping the ball will move, either in the air or off the pitch.

If he is an opening fast bowler who has a third man and no fine leg, he is unlikely to bowl an 'inswinger' (the ball that swings in from the off); alternatively, if there is a fine leg and a short leg, the bowler will probably move it either way. Once you have faced an over from a fast or fast medium bowler you will have noticed whether he bowls sideways on (outswingers), or open-chested (usually inswingers). Final confirmation of which way he is trying to move the ball can be assessed by how his bowling arm follows through – either across his body for the outswinger or down by his side for the opposite delivery. If the bowler is only medium paced, similar actions may indicate off cutters and leg cutters.

If you are facing a spin bowler, your initial thoughts will be to judge how much, and which way, the ball is turning and bouncing.

A study of the field placings will help you to assess this. By observing the bowler carefully, a batsman can begin to read the delivery by the shape of the bowler's delivery position as well as by watching his hand as he releases the ball. Off-spinners will normally bowl around the wicket to a right-handed batsman, but over the wicket to a left-handed batsman, whereas right-handed leg-spinners with their combination of leg spin, top spin and googly, usually bowl over the wicket.

Concentration and patience are key requirements for dealing with a good slow bowler, but feel light on your feet, ready to move. Once you feel confident you can then play your shots and move down the wicket to upset the bowler's length, thus giving yourself more scoring opportunities.

All batsmen should watch the bowler carefully, in case he varies his normal style, usually by a slightly faster or slower delivery.

Take care to look around the fielding positions before the bowler starts to bowl a new over, in case the opposing Captain has quietly changed their positions. Also take note where the best fielders are positioned, do not only note the positions but also the actual players. Watch the bowler to see from where he delivers the ball, and if he suddenly goes wider or even delivers the ball earlier in his run-up. All such deliveries are legitimate ruses to tempt you, the batsman, into making a false shot. Remember he is trying to read you as you are trying to read him.

THINK – Bowling

Fast Bowling – The Mental Approach

The fast bowler is the power of the attack, the 'strike' bowler who has the opportunity to take wickets before the opposing batsmen can establish their innings. As the opening bowler you are the spearhead when your team are fielding. It is your responsibility to gain the initiative over your opponent's batsmen and establish your team's position as being on the offensive, with them on the defensive.

Before you bowl the first ball, your body language, the field you set, will all send out messages to the batting side. It is vital you are accurate and aggressive (even hostile) in your first over. Alternatively if you bowl at half pace and are hit for a few runs and mention you had a heavy night the night before, you will have given the batsmen the opportunity to start 'on the offensive' and it will be your team defending. While the opening exchanges are taking place – finding your 'length' and accuracy, you might start with a square leg, but then after three or four balls bring the fielder up to short leg, which will send danger signals to the batsman. Your job is to create pressure that leads to taking wickets, and above all accuracy counts. This builds pressure steadily, until eventually the batsman's concentration is broken – that is now your chance to breakthrough.

As much as your job is to build the pressure, it is also your responsibility to be able to strike when the batsman cracks. You have to learn to increase and relax pressure and, probably of greatest significance, be aware of these critical moments. Each batsman will have different ways to indicate he has lost patience or is worried about facing you.

Some of the more obvious symptoms are:

- Flashing at balls wide of the off stump
- Becoming frustrated mistiming a shot
- Not being able to score quickly enough

- Declining to run, thus safely remaining at the non-strikers end
- Batting out of character

This last point will only be understood through constant observation during the batsman's innings. Other points to notice are, for instance, if it is not a particularly hot day and the batsman asks for a drink of water, or, he needs a change of gloves.

Another area that is specifically in the fast bowler's armoury, is bowling short fast balls that might hit the batsman if he misses the ball, hence testing his courage. Some batsmen fear the short rising ball and will back away.

It is not a case of continuously bowling this ball, but just occasionally, once you have planted the 'seed of doubt' in the batsman's mind, you have, or should have, the ability to gain his wicket. If fear is in his mind, it will not be long before he makes a 'rash' shot, as his concentration will be on evading the ball rather than selecting the right shot.

An opening batsman might have a tendency to play more off the back foot; you should note this and pitch the ball further up to him. This is in your favour, for the more you pitch the ball up the more it is likely to swing.

All we have stated up to now deals with your opening spell. Your pace, length and direction are designed to penetrate the batsman's defence, before he can settle in. The factor of your pace is another critical item. If when you are rested, there is a great difference in the speed of bowling from the next bowler, the batsman may find it difficult to readjust to his slower pace. On being rested you need to observe and look for the batsman's weaknesses, especially how he handles slow bowling, so that when you return you might try and bowl the slower, surprise ball. While you are not bowling you must regain your strength for when you are asked to bowl again.

This could involve short sharp spells to break a stand, by taking a wicket, or to act as a 'stock' bowler, providing a rest for one of your team-mates. This might be required if the pitch is a spinner's wicket and the team's spinner needs a rest. It may make the batsman readjust twice in a space of a few overs. So you must continue to concentrate, relax your muscles, keep warm, and learn as much as you can before returning to the attack.

If you are a swing bowler and find the ball is not swinging, you must remember that the ball may only swing at certain temperatures or humidity – specific climatic conditions. In consequence it is your **thinking** that takes over, so try bowling a little faster or a little slower. Other factors you should consider are your body position on delivery: how you are holding the ball and your follow through. All of which are vital for an appropriate end result…the best in these conditions.

But while you are looking for the correct end result you must be very careful that your own body language gives nothing away to the batsman, who should be watching you as carefully as you are watching him.

Aggressive attitudes in the follow through and glaring at the batsman – eyeball to eyeball, and telling him that he cannot bat are undesirable aspects of cricket. In any case you may well undo your own situation rather than his. If he regularly opens the innings he may, sadly, be used to such behaviour!

In fact excessive aggression could increase his concentration and instantly improve his performance, therefore being counter productive.

However, if your delivery surprises him, or even hits him, his mental attitude may be affected by a casual remark, within his earshot, such as 'It's surprising that one got through as the pitch is slow today!'

The next ball he will expect another fast delivery so try bowling a slower ball but make sure he has to play it.

Finally if you are bowling at a tail-ender and you only need to finish off the last two wickets, vary your pace and make sure the batsman has to play **every** ball. Sometimes you may give him a ball to hit for four, because all tail end batsmen like scoring runs. The next delivery is your chance to strike as you might have lulled him into a false sense of security.

Slow Bowling – Or Ensuring Batsmen Self-Destruct

Of all the disciplines in cricket slow bowling is the most demanding and one of the most rewarding parts of the game. A slow bowler, whether a spinner or a floater of the ball, has to invest all his mental effort into working out batsmen, recognising their weaknesses and imposing a control over them which will ultimately result in the taking of their wicket.

Consider the vital requirements of slow bowling:

- Confidence
- Patience
- Accuracy - The ability to bowl a good line and length
- To be flexible and adaptable when bowling to various batsmen
- To try not to have **too** many variations
- Concentration
- Accept that batsmen will get the better of you on a specific day, but be able to return with confidence as soon as required
- Knowledge of the Laws of the game
- Respect for the umpire; irritating the umpire with excessive and ignorant appealing will not further your cause
- Good understanding with your Captain

The first point, confidence, is of paramount importance, especially when you start your spell. In order that you can have such confidence you need the support of your Captain, because it is surprising how many captains can undermine your confidence, through his or her own failure to judge your character. He has asked you to bowl and, even being a good cricketer, may lack the thought or intuition to give you total support. Any

I'm sure somebody was moving behind the bowler's arm.

sign of disagreement in front of the batsman, increases the batsman's confidence whilst undermining that of the bowler.

You will have been coached in the basic method of slow bowling, but there is much to learn. You will continue to learn throughout your cricketing life, because this art is enjoyable and providing you remain fit you can be a slow bowler for 40 years or more.

Learning to be **accurate** is vital; you cannot hope to be of any use to your side if you bowl one or two bad balls each over which go for runs and take the pressure off the batsman. Accuracy comes from practice, which in turn creates confidence. Until you can pitch the ball five times out of six onto a saucer-sized area on a good length there is no point in introducing into your bowling the other skills of variety, flight and guile.

If you are a spin bowler, rather than a slow swing bowler (floater), you are unlikely to open the bowling, so you will be in the field for a while before the Captain asks you to bowl. This is not time wasted, because you will be studying the performance of the pitch and of the batsman.

You will have determined the wind direction, the slopes in the outfield, which boundary is nearer and which end bounces the most. Stay calm, put all these factors into your mind and be ready when the call comes. Your Captain will be eager to have you bowling if he knows you are confident and ready to perform. All bowlers, especially slow bowlers, should know how to be able to read a batsman.

From the moment he takes his stance, notice how he holds the bat and his ability or non-ability to use his feet. Observe his awareness of the fielding positions you have set and the deliberate gaps to which you want him to try and hit the ball. Take note of what 'guard' the batsman takes, it might indicate whether he is stronger on his leg side or making off-side strokes. See if he has an open or closed stance. Notice whether his top hand has the back of the hand facing towards cover point or in the arc around to your bowling position. This may indicate that he likes driving. Alternatively, if the back of the hand is facing the slips, he is more likely to be a defensive player.

Now you are bowling. You and your Captain have jointly set the fielding positions, thanks partly to your earlier observance of the batsman's techniques; start your spell by searching for the ideal length and bowl straight to make the batsman play the ball.

All batsmen feel safer if they do not have to play a shot at the early deliveries from a new bowler, so do not give him the chance of watching the ball go by. As you settle into your rhythm start to explore the possible response from the pitch and begin to offer your opponent some variety. The mental battle has begun. Tease the batsman with subtle changes of pace; vary your grip, and flight the ball, putting it above the batsman's eye line to deceive him in the air.

You want him to be attempting to attack you. Eventually he will fail to read the flight or the spin and his error will be his downfall. Your perseverance has been rewarded with a wicket.

Pitch the ball to land on the leg side and see if his head drops to the off when he hits the ball, as he is then likely to give a catch to mid-wicket.

When you bowl outside the off stump see if he wants to play it. Then see how far you can make him play away from his body, as the farther he goes the more likely he is to edge it. Ascertain whether he prefers to play forward or back, **but**, never bowl really short of a length. If you find the batsman attempts to superimpose his ability over yours, lead him to do all the work.

If wickets are not coming keep bowling tightly, using your stock ball. It pays as with 'playing-in' a fish to encourage the batsman to have to be more adventurous, so that he is less likely to remain for long.

Now the new batsman has arrived, he is nervous and tentative at the start of his innings; again, bowl straight and make him play with his bat from the first ball. If the ball is turning and there is a degree of bounce you will probably pressure him by placing close fielders around his bat.

Alternatively, if you bowl floaters you can tempt him to drive early in his innings, and then it is better to let him have freedom near the bat and set your fielders further back.

After several overs test him with a few positional changes in the field and start varying your deliveries. Observe his technique, for as he needs to pick up the run rate, his impatience could be his undoing and his wicket fall. Always try and draw the batsman forward and make him drive at the ball; short balls will not take wickets but will concede runs. All this is known as 'reading the batsman'.

It has generally been thought that slow bowlers cannot contain good batsmen. However, even on a good pitch, by bowling to your well-placed field and maintaining your accuracy you will be harder to score runs off than the fast man. On really good batting surfaces all bowlers have to think defensively, because run scoring is so much easier. The tendency today is to bowl flatter (reduce your loop), keep it tight and wait for the batsman to make the mistake.

Make sure your key fielders are in the correct positions, this is always vital, as it will add the pressure on the batsman.

Use your brain and bowl to a good player's weakness, block off his favourite shots and entice him into hitting across the line of flight. Talk with your wicket-keeper, who may have noticed something that you have missed. Make a plan together to unsettle the batsman with a different approach.

Endeavour to work out specific gaps to entice the batsman to make shots that put him at risk. For example, if you bowl the ball that leaves the bat, open a wide gap at mid-wicket and encourage him to hit across the line you are bowling, making it likely he will edge the ball. It will go higher in the air the harder he tries to hit it.

You need to work out your stock ball (the one you can bowl at will) and the line you are most likely to cause problems for the batsman.

You must be able to bowl a slower ball or a faster one, be able to change your line by small variables, so the batsman fails to understand he is under your control.

You must learn the art of delivering the ball above the 'eye' line, which is especially valuable when you have a strong hitter facing you. You may have to shorten the 'length' of your bowling for a ball, but follow it with a faster ball of good length, or a 'yorker'.

You can learn to control the ball on any piece of ground, on the beach, or by using a ball against a wall. Mark out a variety of four-inch squares and pitch the ball at them; the better you become the sooner you learn the art of bowling.

You must learn to disguise your variations, such as by gripping the ball differently, slowing your arm speed, running in quicker or slower.

Think of using the width of the crease, bowling the ball from further away, or closer to the batsman. All these variations must be practised to perfection.

Although you need to be able to vary your bowling, only do it occasionally. The batsman may concentrate on every delivery, which you wish to discourage, but you want him to think he has worked you out, so lull him into a false sense of security, and then you can surprise him.

Consider small variations, such as bowling a little wider, with a slightly higher 'loop' or slightly faster and flatter – but while doing any of these changes you must be able to remain very accurate.

Unless you are a spinner who creates 'lots' of turn, observers will not understand how you obtain your victims, so leave them in suspense – a magician never explains how he does his tricks.

Whilst bearing in mind what has been said it is important that you continue to liaise with your Captain. The Captain makes the final decision and he will advise as to whether runs must be restricted or whether it is worth giving some runs away in return for picking up several wickets. Sometimes one must run the risk of losing a game in order to win it, but that is the Captain's responsibility.

As you become an experienced and respected slow bowler you may find wickets harder to take. Usually this is because batsmen get to know you and your various mysterious deliveries, which means they take fewer risks against you.

To overcome this try and bowl in tandem with another good, accurate bowler so that both ends are tied up and the batsmen have to attempt to break the shackles or become runless.

Always watch your fielders; they are inclined to roam and not be where you put them, so a quick check is necessary at the beginning of each over, or after a wicket has fallen.

Slow bowling makes an elegant and attractive contribution to the wonderful game of cricket and many of its purveyors, including your authors, have spent years weaving a web of intrigue. The demands of patience and mental output are very good for the character.

Summary

Once you have established yourself as a slow bowler and developed the various techniques we have discussed, it is then time to consider certain other factors to make you the complete cricketer.

For instance, on very good pitches one has to be more patient. You might find all the playing conditions are against you.

Often at the beginning of an English season, pitches will be wet, slow and provide little bounce, making it easier for the batsman to stay in.

What are your options? You must try to bowl slower, give the ball more 'air' and tempt the batsman into lunging at the ball on the front foot and possibly hitting the ball in the air. He could also overbalance and be stumped.

When pitches become harder and truer, then you will need to bowl a little faster. With a firmer pitch you may gain an exaggerated bounce. If this is the case, then carry on, because the more bounce you achieve the more effective you will become.

On occasions you will not bowl well, then reduce your variations and bowl as tightly as you can and depend on your 'stock' ball.

If you find a batsman is hitting you straight for fours make certain you put your fielders deeper to protect the boundary. If you then give the ball 'air' and he hits you for one or more sixes, ensure he is drawn down the wicket to the pitch of the ball. You subtly reduce the length of the ball, which hides the fact that you are bowling the ball even slower. This takes real courage and confidence, but the batsman then has to put all the pace on the ball with his shot.

Try and bowl a 'line' to one side, as it is easier to contain a batsman by having most of your fielders on a specific side of the field.

Remember when you are bowling to a big hitter who has a good eye, concentrate on bowling a full length at his feet. This restricts his hitting arc by reducing the swing of his arms.

If you are a slow bowler who entices batsmen to leave the security of their crease and take the attack to you, work out a system with your wicket-keeper to beat the batsman and have him stumped.

THINK – Fielding Positions

Arrows on field placings refer to alternative fielding positions.

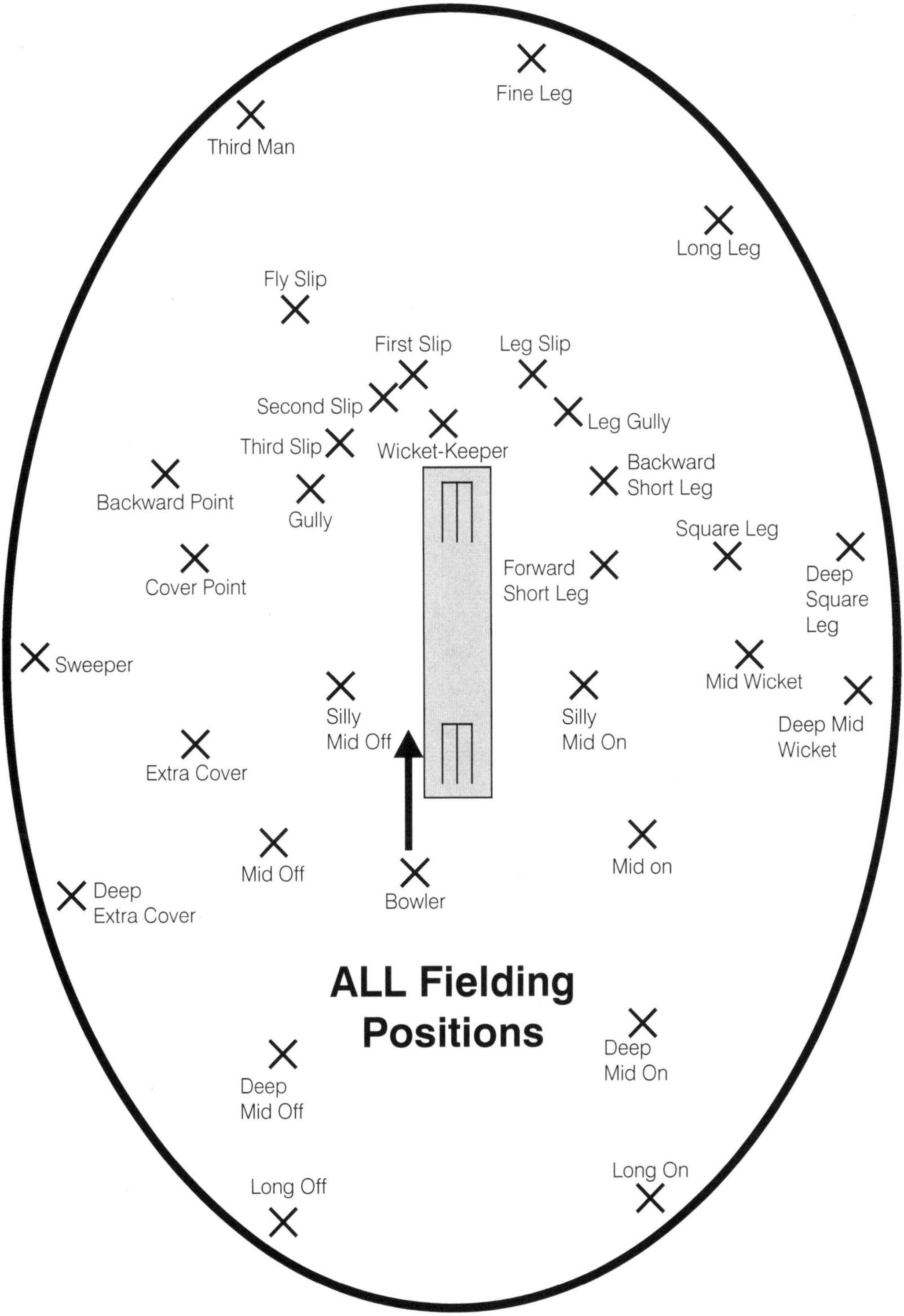
Fine Leg
Third Man
Long Leg
Fly Slip
First Slip
Leg Slip
Second Slip
Leg Gully
Third Slip
Wicket-Keeper
Backward Short Leg
Backward Point
Gully
Square Leg
Cover Point
Forward Short Leg
Deep Square Leg
Sweeper
Mid Wicket
Silly Mid Off
Silly Mid On
Deep Mid Wicket
Extra Cover
Mid Off
Mid on
Bowler
Deep Extra Cover
ALL Fielding Positions
Deep Mid On
Deep Mid Off
Long On
Long Off

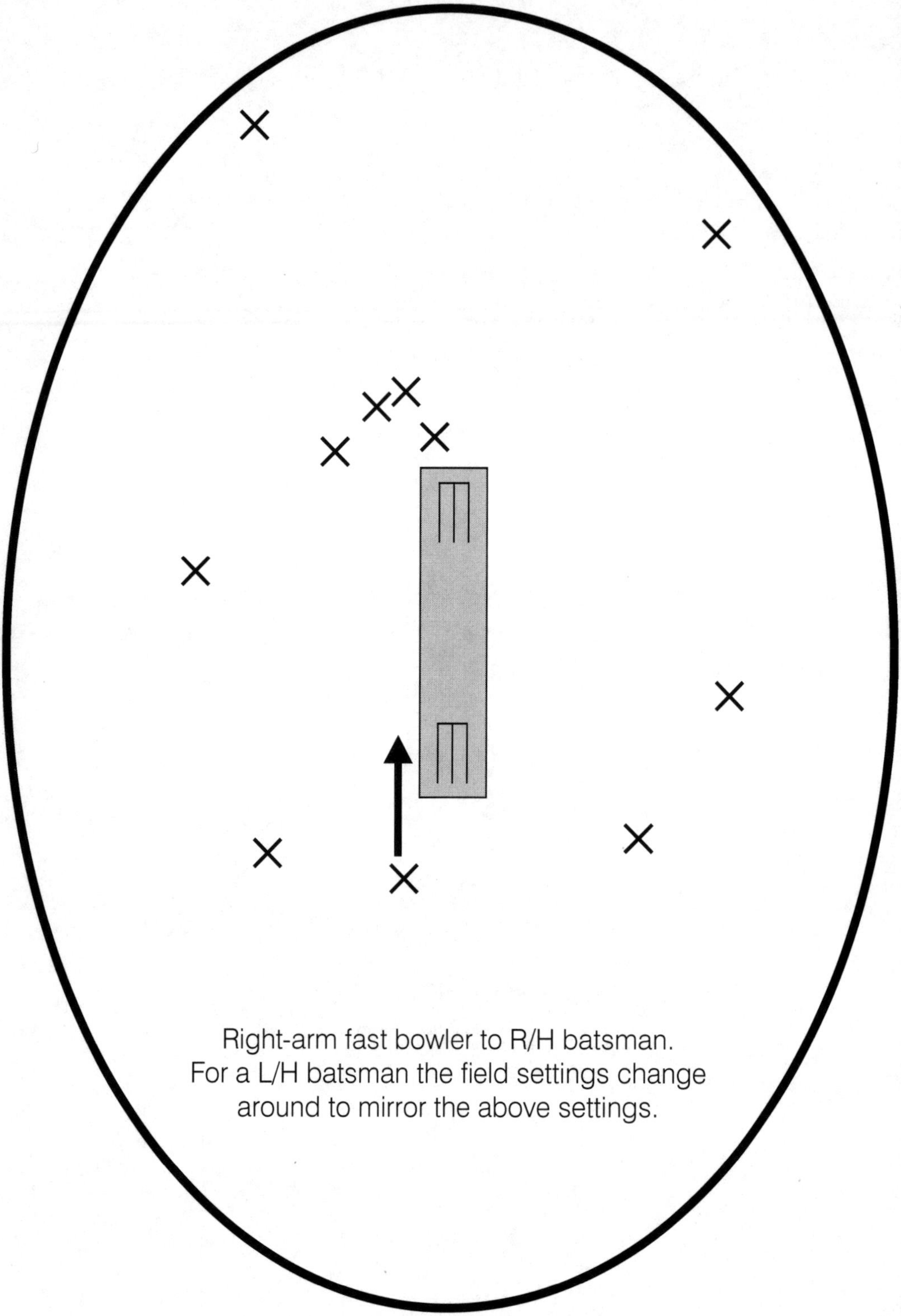

Right-arm fast bowler to R/H batsman.
For a L/H batsman the field settings change
around to mirror the above settings.

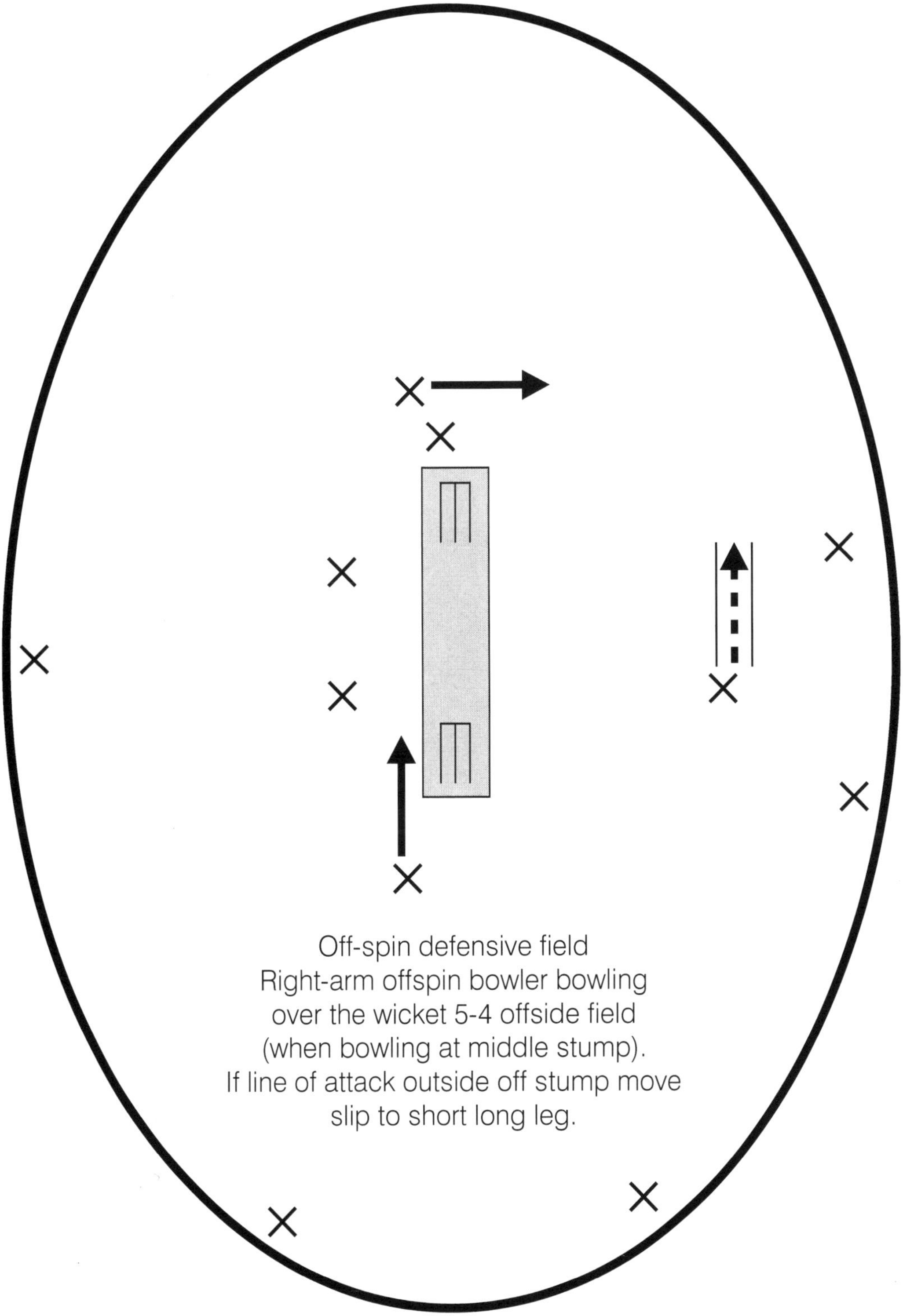

Off-spin defensive field
Right-arm offspin bowler bowling
over the wicket 5-4 offside field
(when bowling at middle stump).
If line of attack outside off stump move
slip to short long leg.

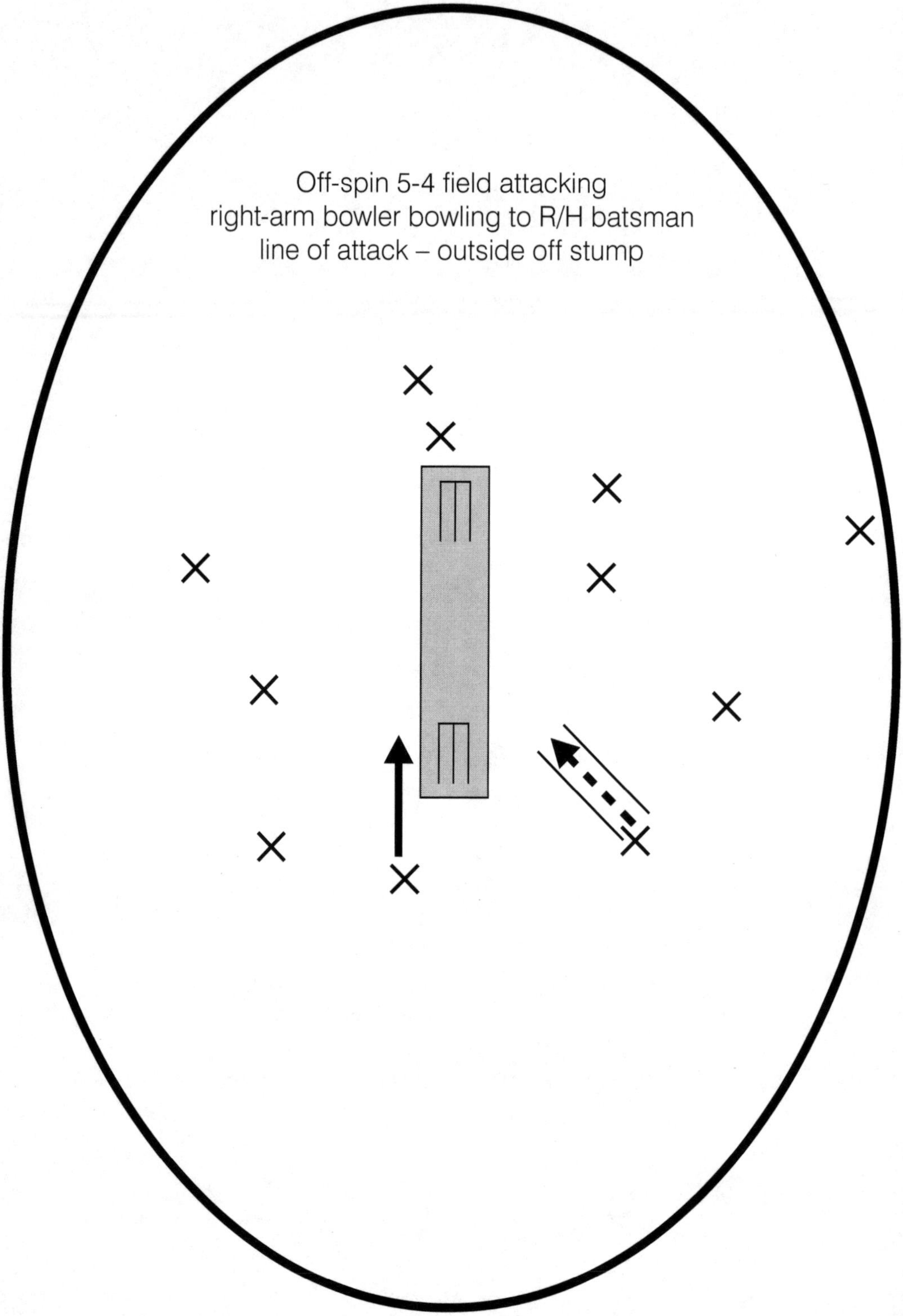
Off-spin 5-4 field attacking
right-arm bowler bowling to R/H batsman
line of attack – outside off stump

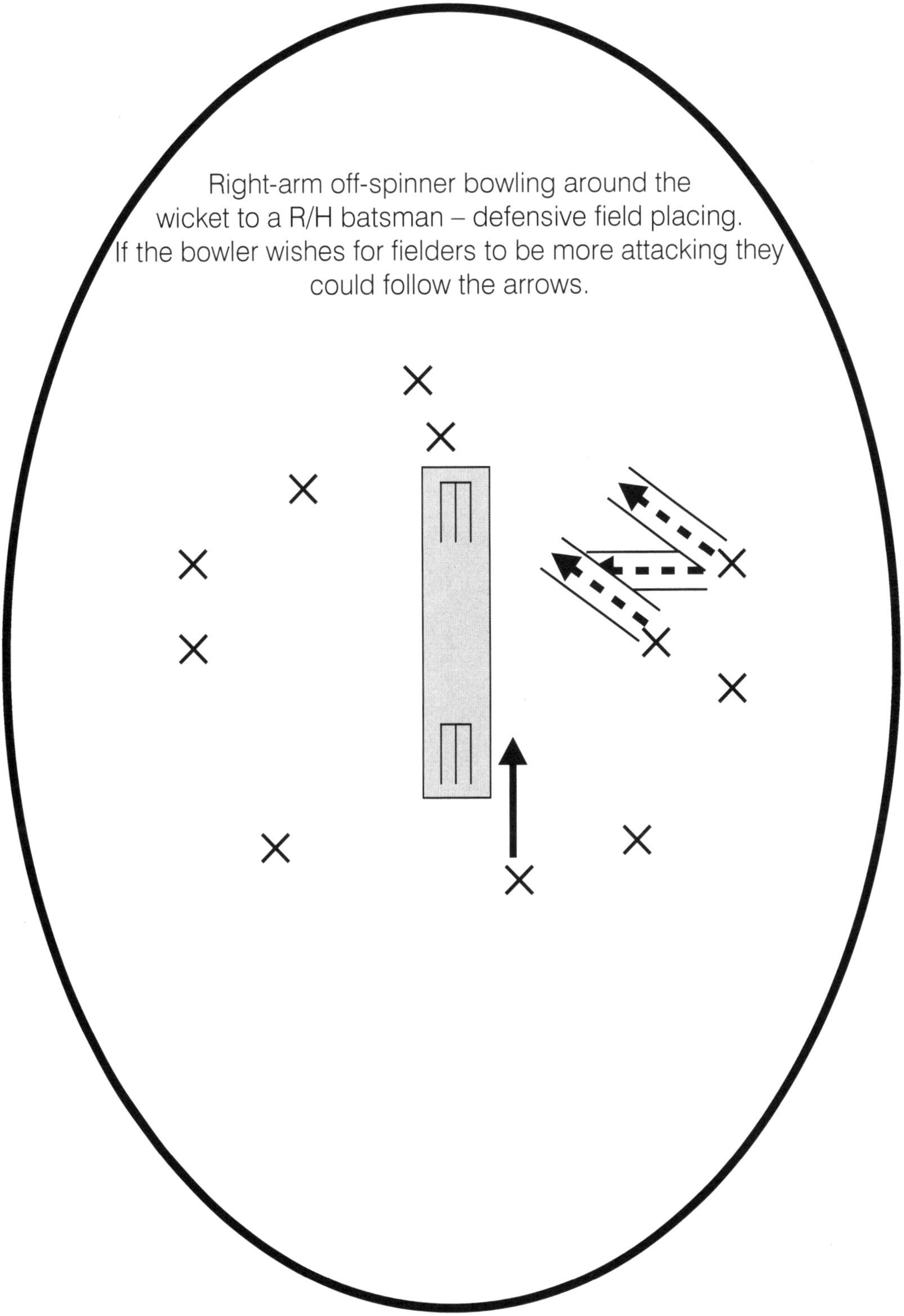

Right-arm off-spinner bowling around the wicket to a R/H batsman – defensive field placing. If the bowler wishes for fielders to be more attacking they could follow the arrows.

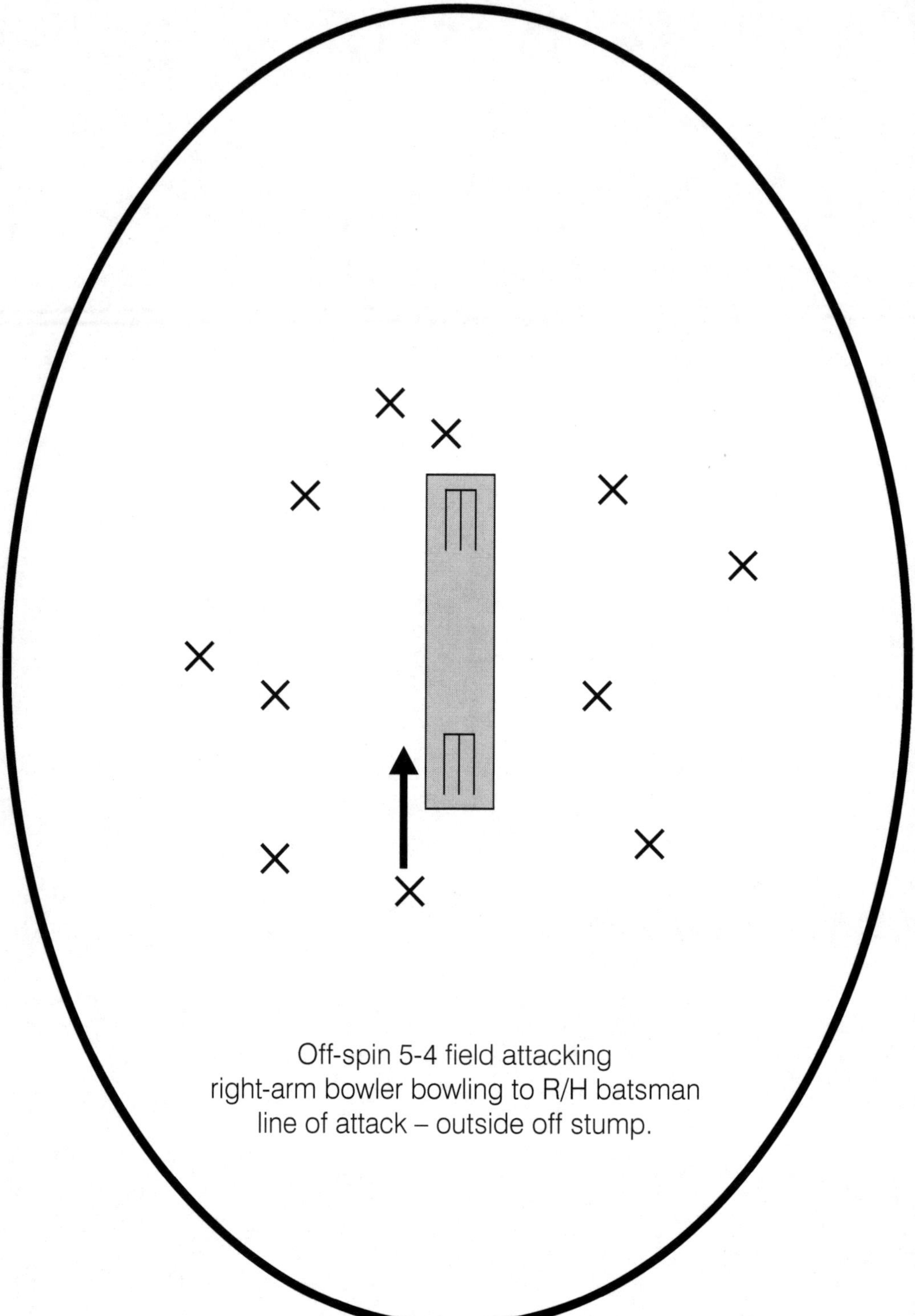

Off-spin 5-4 field attacking
right-arm bowler bowling to R/H batsman
line of attack – outside off stump.

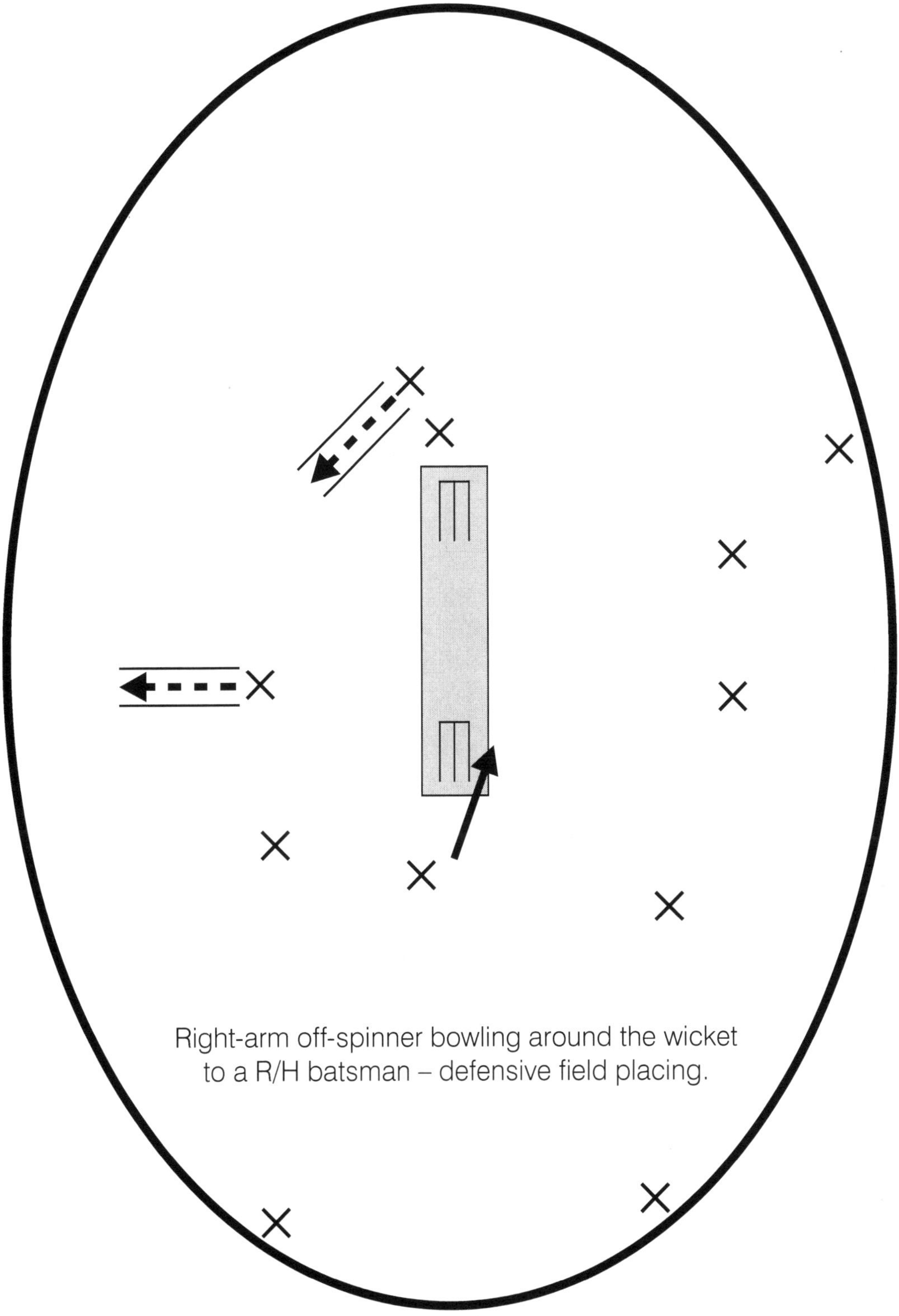

Right-arm off-spinner bowling around the wicket to a R/H batsman – defensive field placing.

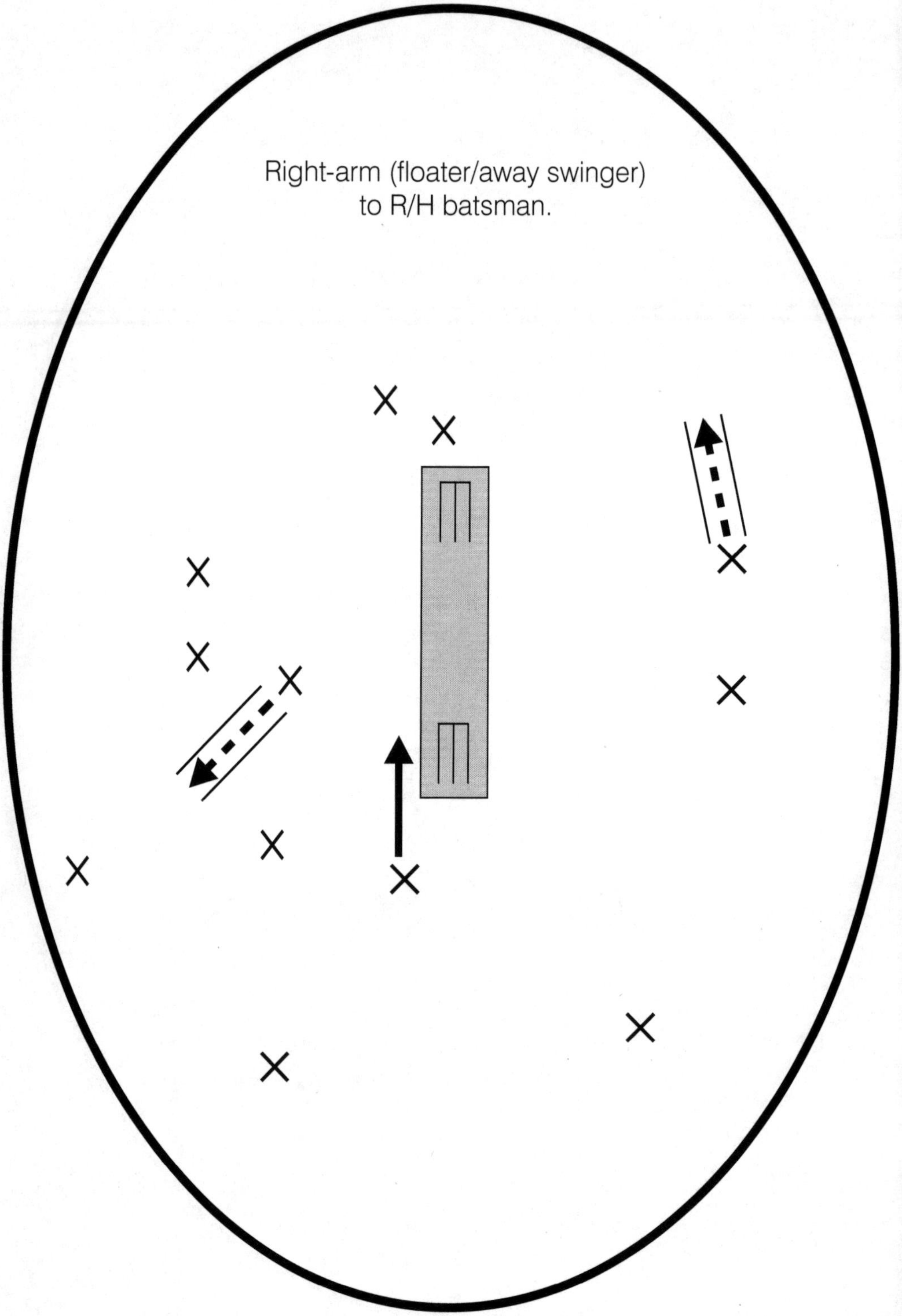
Right-arm (floater/away swinger)
to R/H batsman.

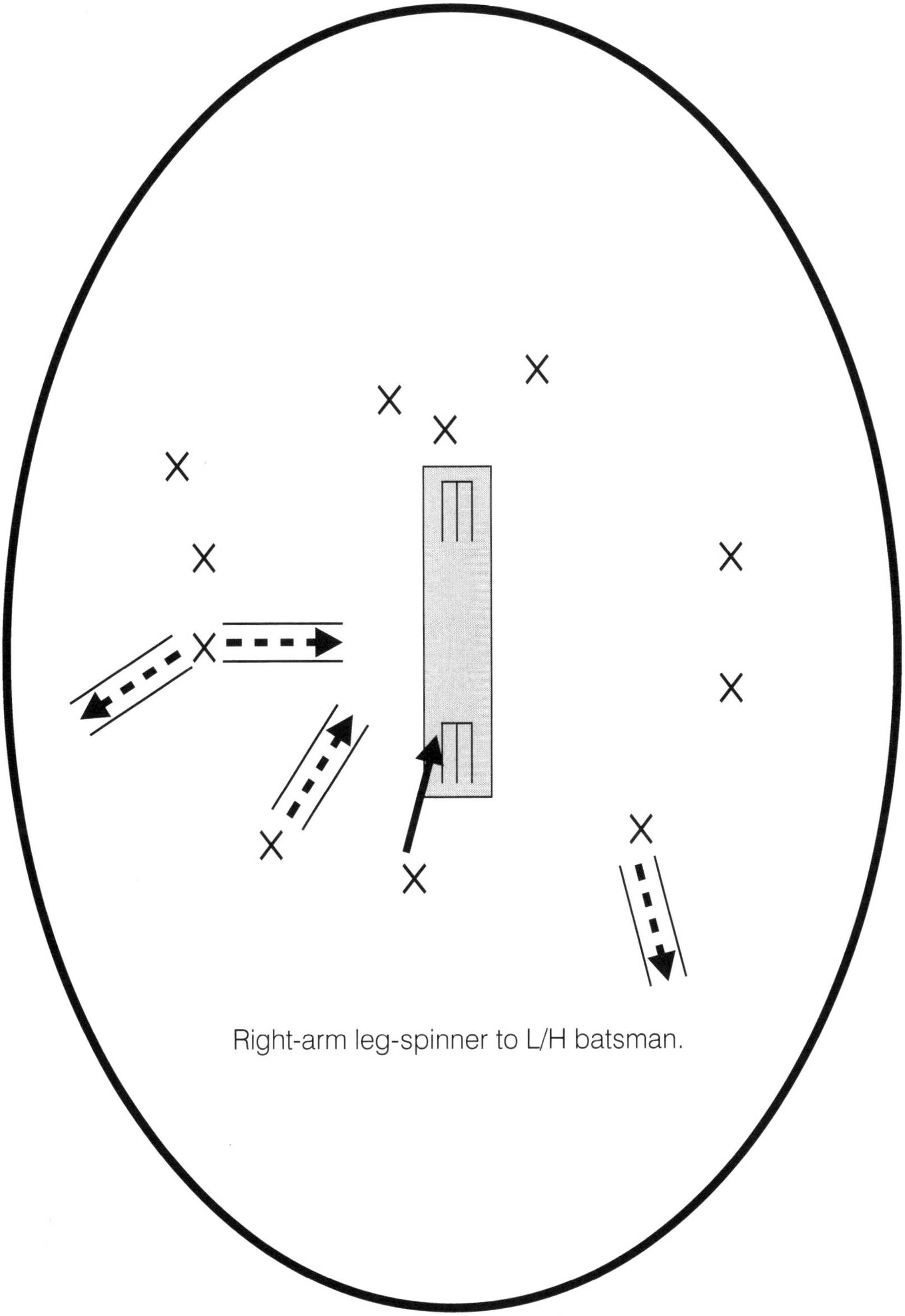

Right-arm leg-spinner to L/H batsman.

THINK – Fielding

This section is about the mental approach to the art of fielding and the various fielding positions.

Every fielding position requires the following attributes:

- Fitness
- Good reactions
- Concentration
- Courage
- Anticipation
- Judgement of ball speed
- Alertness

The more you practise the better you will become and the more adaptable you will be as a member of the team.

Just remember that you may be a batsman or you maybe a bowler but all ten members of the team are fielders.

Whichever position you field in at any time in the match you should look at the Captain between every ball that is bowled, in case he wishes to move you, this saves time and can be sometimes achieved without the batsman being aware of the change.

Fielding Close To The Bat

The slips, gully, silly point, short leg and bat/pad positions in front of the batsman all require sharp reactions. A fielder's batting experience will alert him to the likelihood of a catch, and such anticipation can give him more time to take a catch.

Gauging where to stand for each type of bowler will only come with

I'd rather be fielding on the boundary.

experience. This will depend on the speed of the ball, whether a new ball or softer old ball, on the hardness of the pitch and whether the batsman is attacking or defending. It will also depend on the amount of swing or turn, and the bowler's line and length. Be prepared to practise with a catching aid.

Chris Old who was an outstanding close catcher for Yorkshire and England says, 'Close catching is a state of mind.'*

All the best close catchers in the world are **relaxed in body** and **alert in mind**. If you can adopt and maintain this mental and physical state you will very rarely flinch. Flinching causes loss of rhythm, poor movement, and breakdown in technique, and a tense close catcher will drop or miss more catches than he or she takes. By being relaxed and alert more time may be created to execute a well-timed movement with good technique to catch the ball with soft hands.

*(G.V. Palmer, ECB Coaching Course – Specialist Close Catching, 2001).

Fielding – Saving One Run

Cover point, extra-cover, mid-wicket and square leg are all positions where the players need to be very mobile and quick off the mark.

The first objective is to stop the ball, and a mobile, alert fielder will often deter the batsman from risking a run. Move ten to fifteen paces every time the ball is bowled, and react to the shape of the batsman's stroke (soft or hard hit).

When there is a call for a sharp single but your alertness causes the batsmen to hesitate and a shout of no rings out, always throw to the end opposite the no. There is more chance of a run out at that end. Think about it and work it out.

The fielders in these positions should always be aware which batsman is the faster runner between the wickets, who turns the faster and who turns blind. This makes them aware as to which set of stumps they should throw to should there be a chance of a run out. However, when fielding at cover or mid-wicket, consider throwing the ball underarm. The time saved winding up can sometimes make up for loss of power. In any case, it will make the batsman think twice about attempting such a run. In most cases it will be to the end to which the batsman who hit the ball is running, as he has further to run, rather than towards the non-striker, who can back up as the bowler delivers the ball.

Backing Up

The fielders in this inner ring will be responsible for backing up these instant fielding activities and preventing overthrows. Therefore you must watch the ball all the time, even if you are not the actual fielder of the shot.

Boundary Fielding

The best runners and longest throwers will be the most likely fielders to patrol the boundaries. Again it is vital to be mobile.

Consider being a few paces in from the boundary so as to intercept the ball earlier, and possibly prevent two runs being scored. But never field where a ball over your head bounces inside the boundary.

You must be able to back track or turn round and take the ball over your shoulder, whilst **continuing to keep your eyes on the ball** the whole time – essential if you are to take a catch right on the boundary edge.

The law allows a fielder to start walking in from outside the boundary, so when the batsman hits the ball you are already on the move. Of course, you must be inside the field of play as the bowler delivers the ball.

Always use two hands to stop the ball in the outfield; a half stop often results in the ball still reaching the boundary, for you have insufficient time and space to recover from your error.

Remember that long flatter throws with one bounce will be more accurate than those thrown on the full, and reach the wicket-keeper more quickly; do not be ashamed to use this method.

Summary

Today's television coverage of cricket shows many good exhibitions of fielding. Watch and see how quick, accurate fielding saves runs and sometimes takes wickets. Enjoy your fielding and become an indispensable member of your team.

THINK – Wicket-keeping

The wicket-keeper is the fulcrum of every team in the field. The success of every bowler will at various times be balanced by the 'keeper's ability and performance. He is the 'hub' at the centre of the game to whom most fielders will return the ball. He can make or destroy a match. Hence he has a vital role to play, his thinking and seeing role is very valuable to all bowlers as well as to his Captain. His knowledge and experience will determine the positioning of the close fielders. He, most of all, will probably be the first to 'read' the batsman.

His first thoughts will be to gauge the atmospheric conditions and their effect on the pitch, and how much bounce each end will realise according to the bowler's speed. This will determine how far back he will stand, thus influencing the aforementioned close fielders. He must convey to his team confidence, enthusiasm and support. He has to find the best ways to do this without undermining their confidence. All these factors are part of his thought process throughout the opposition's innings. He has to **think** about his team-mates, he has to concentrate and **think** about his own job, which is continuous. The role these days requires far more 'chat', to his slip cordon, to the bowler and fielders, but of greatest importance, to his Captain. Every little movement before, during and after the batsman makes a shot or even 'leaves' the ball, should be recorded in the 'keeper's memory. Depending on how well he knows his bowlers, he might have to set up a system of signals or know when a fast bowler is likely to bowl a slower ball.

For the spin bowler or 'floater' he will need to know how the bowler reacts to a batsman leaving his crease.

He has to think about where the sun is shining, as the fielders throwing from that side must understand it is better if the ball bounces before reaching him, so he can see it more easily.

The wicket-keeper is on a hiding whenever he 'dons' the gloves, because he must assume that every ball that is bowled will finish in his hands. His thought process and reactions have to be lightning quick. From the time the ball leaves the bowler's hand, and its arrival with him, he has to instantly decide whether he takes it outside the off stump or has to go to the leg side. His brain must act in a fraction of a second, whilst also estimating any variations that might be caused if the batsman edges it. Furthermore he must assess the bounce of the ball, so that with regular concentration he will be reading its line ready perhaps to dive in front of the slips or alternatively to run twenty metres in any direction to take a skied catch.

All this requires complete concentration on every ball – the way it leaves the bowler's hand, its flight, and the exact spot on which it pitches – and yet, though alert, he **must be relaxed**, and not tense.

An experienced wicket-keeper may often be able to anticipate the movement of the ball or even sometimes guess at the batsman's stroke selection and ability to hit the ball. Some batsmen move across the line of the ball more than others, and the 'keeper needs to adjust his stance and his head accordingly. As previously emphasised, concentration is needed to respond to all unexpected occurrences within the crease.

When all this works well the 'keeper's performance may not even be noticed, but when it doesn't his weakness will stand out like a sore thumb.

Who would be a wicket-keeper! If he does his job well then he is a cricketer and a very valuable member of the team and he should be your first selection. If he can bat as well that is an even greater asset. If your 'keeper is a player who is both knowledgeable and well experienced it would seem reasonable to let him lead your appeals, though occasionally the batsman may block his view of the ball after it has pitched. It is accepted that a large part of appealing is based on reactions by the 'keeper, whose attitude needs to be intelligent if the team is to be taken seriously by the umpire. He should restrict his appeals to a genuine belief that the ball may have hit the wicket – and gain the umpire's respect and thus the likelihood of a favourable decision!

THINK – Learning

The whole process of learning starts earlier than ever nowadays and it is a brave individual who can suggest when that time comes. However, it must be for the parent or possibly the teacher, to decide. For children with any natural ball sense it is likely to be three or four years of age, with simple games starting the process.

Most children want to play with balloons at first, with kicking a ball as the next likely development. Parents wishing to have a child ahead of its contemporaries should move in at this stage and see how their child is developing both physically and mentally. It is important to note that the learning state is at its pinnacle in the first five years of their lives, so progress gained in these formative stages will be valuable and will stand the young person in good stead as compared with those who leave it too late.

The learning stage must however be FUN as all children have a short concentration span. Parents who press too hard for the sporting prowess of their offspring can find that there is a sudden loss of keenness.

There is much of interest in the world to tempt today's youngsters and, in the end, it is the child who will choose which sport (if any) that he wants to pursue.

THINK – Training

The methods of Training depend on the specific coach leading the programme, attitudes differ across a wide spectrum, according to which country the training is taking place.

Most agree that every exponent must be fit, athletic and agile, prior to taking the field. Still there is a prominence in preparation of the physical rather than the mental state. This author would suggest that each go hand-in-hand. In fact, if the individual is mentally prepared and knowledgeable for what requirements are needed for his physique and the process in gaining the end result, then the achievement is more likely to be reached.

Targets must be set at each part of the development, so that individuals are able to recognise the progress each step delivers them forward.

To **THINK fitness** will give the individual a well being to improve their whole attitude to life, once attained he will want to stay in this aura and **THINK – Training** will become a way of life rather than that of a necessary chore.

Many young people believe their youthful energy will be enough, those days are long gone. To be at the top of your sport you must make every effort to have as complete a fitness programme as is possible, you then have the platform to progress in your given sport.

Any ache, strain, injury or pain will minimise your effectiveness – to achieve, the mind must be totally concentrating on the achievement of your goal.

When preparing the young for training, it should be remembered that a young mind does not have the same concentration pattern as an adult, nor the ability to concentrate at length. It is necessary therefore to break up training periods into short, sharp time spans, bring fun and competitiveness into each and every section of the activity.

During the period of growing up there are a huge number of possible distractions, especially competing with the hours required for training.

It is our belief that if the youth understands the mindset behind the physical needs as well as the partial and complete benefits attainable, then they will be far more willing to participate and reach out for the goal for which they are aiming.

Training includes all factors of preparation, initially from the earliest age through school and university to adulthood, sometimes for the next match, other occasions for a new season, a different team or standard.

There is individual personal training as well as team development.

Training the mind will include reading instructional literature, books on the art, achieved in different ways, by former great cricketers, and how great matches were won and lost.

With many of the international teams there are coaches and team trainers mapping every shot, the bowling actions and the playing of each ball bowled and how fielders field the ball. This will help each player to map his or her own reaction to each situation. Within this scenario opposition will be analysed before each match, so teams can gain the best advantage when facing each opponent batsman or bowler.

Even within the top leagues there is more software available for coaches to assess their opponents, which is sure to follow their professional peers.

Most coaching schools have videos to study a batsman's technique – and there are 'speed guns' to measure the pace at which each bowler operates.

THINK – Practice

It is vital all cricketers at all ages practise their game.

Practice makes perfect is an old adage, but without it you will never be a good cricketer.

Every department of the game needs practising and as we have stated before it is important to think and plan your practice NOT just go into the nets and play at practising. A proper plan should be adopted.

Parents or Teachers: If you are the parent you must first think of your own commitment, have you the time, the means of transport to ferry the child to and from practice, be there to encourage, if need be participate and be supportive for the preparation and after training, for the 'homework' activity?

If you have a child who is showing interest and ability in cricket, whilst its development is such that the mental/physical is not likely to be damaged through following a training pattern, then you would be well advised to seek professional help. The England & Wales Cricket Board (Lord's Cricket Ground, London) has Cricket Development Officers in every county; in turn they have professional coaches available to offer you the information you need.

Take a professional stance yourself, provide the authority with as much information about the youth as possible.

Offer a profile – name, picture, plus height, weight, school, the number of years having an interest and playing cricket, age, number of siblings and whether they are interested as well. If you are the parent, your knowledge and experience – all these factors that can be harnessed for the development of the child. If the child has had some coaching already, who was the coach? And what are the coach's qualifications?

For if your child has ball sense, has the desire to play, it is sad if they are to be denied the opportunity which might shape their whole future.

As a person matures, then they must take on the responsibility themselves to set out their own aims and ambitions, take advice from professionals as how to achieve and the pattern of training, practice and development.

When young, it is so easy to follow good intentioned people who might be successful players themselves, but not with the professional knowledge of how to train young limbs or develop ability.

At this stage it is very important to **THINK clothing** and **equipment**.

Clothing should be loose fitting, but does not need to be expensive, for the young quickly grow and need larger sizes. Footwear needs to be comfortable, but needs to include a sole that grips and protects ankles. Buy cricket socks (Horizon will wash and keep shape and can be worn for years), Do Not buy just plimsolls, for they offer no protection. Boys need a 'box' (protective support), all children need helmets by Law to play cricket.

Equipment – please, please do not equip the child with cricket gear that is too big or heavy, for it will reduce ability, risk injury and deter the child from their enjoyment. Most manufacturers make equipment from very small sizes, AGAIN obtain professional advice if in any doubt and do not leave it to the child, because they always try and buy too heavy a bat.

Protection at all ages is vital, a simple injury can easily deter a young child or youth from continuing to support the game, take pain seriously.

Make sure early season practice hardens hands, minimum pain leads to confidence and enjoyment.

The very young should only play with soft balls – tennis or plastic, so they are not frightened of being hurt, more people have turned away from cricket because they were hurt by a cricket ball early in their playing career, than from any other cause.

Net practice – take care that young cricketers are supervised in the net situation, for it can be a captive situation and people bowling in the net to a youngster can easily frighten the batsman.Early practice sessions with those learning at the start of playing cricket are better to have throw-downs.

For training adults and teenagers – the method to gain confidence and improve stroke play can be attained by 'Grooving' shots with throw-downs or the use of a bowling machine.

Training/Practice/Learning should concentrate on all facets of the game, not just batting – bowling and fielding are also vital, with the latter – one should practise picking the ball up, throwing and catching – both distance catches, close catches and hitting a single stump on the run.

Concentration and relaxation are two mental factors that need practising this should include training the memory.

THINK – Concentration

...And Relax

At any stage in our life, whatever we are doing, we must learn to concentrate and relax, the better we learn to do each, then we will be the better for it.

This is very close to the theme of this book. Every aspect of playing cricket well requires the individual to concentrate. The length of the period of concentration will be determined by the length of the match, the length of an innings, but it would be very hard to maintain concentration all the time, so it is necessary to learn how to relax in between the periods of concentration.

All aspects of the game require each individual to concentrate, probably the hardest task is the fielding Captain, as he has to think for his team, each bowler, the positioning of the fielders and the overall state of the game and, whether ALL the team are both involved and not becoming bored. For instance, has somebody been on the boundary and inactive for too long, are the batsmen being played in – rather than being challenged, and while all this is going through his mind, he must concentrate on his own game.

For it is inexcusable to miss a catch or miss a fielding opportunity because he was thinking that a bowling change should be made. The close fielders must concentrate on every ball bowled, must be ready to back up balls thrown in from the boundary or the other side of the pitch, they should also watch the batsman to observe his weaknesses and strengths, this is particularly vital for the wicket-keeper, who should be helping both his Captain and each bowler. Each bowler must concentrate on where he is going to pitch the ball to deliver the ball to create the batsman to make his mistake, for the bowler it is from the start of each over that he should be making the most concentration. However, every bowler should concentrate on each batsman, even when he is not bowling, to ascertain weaknesses for when he is called upon to bowl, each factor must be stored in his memory.

This is probably the one thing the batsman has in common with the bowler, for the batsman should have the memory as to where the fielders are placed, and have some idea as to the type of ball to be bowled.

THINK – Concentration for Fielders

Specific Positions and what to think about:

1. Slips and wicket-keeper – 1st, 2nd slips concentrate on the ball from when it leaves the bowler's hand, they will have noticed the guard the batsman took, how he picks the bat up and whether he plays the ball away from his body. They should also know if the bowler can swing the ball away from the batsman or bowl a leg cutter. If only one slip is in position to a slow bowler he will need to read the bowler's hand to be ready to react to an edge.

   For 3rd and 4th slip and gully fielders, they watch the bat and must be aware to notice whether the batsman moves his feet to the pitch of the ball, especially when driving the ball. If he cuts the ball and the pace of the bowler will determine how square or fine he should position himself unless specifically positioned by Captain or bowler. Having pre-knowledge of the batsman will help to guide him. The Slips and gulley remain in the game till the ball is dead, supporting the wicket-keeper.

   The wicket-keeper must concentrate on every ball bowled as even if the batsman makes no shot he will have to collect the ball. If the ball is hit then he must be ready to either receive the ball from the fielder and/or be aware of each aspect of his responsibilities, one of which is to keep the fielders on their toes and competitive. But to do his job well he needs to notice how well the batsman plays, how well the bowler bowls and report all to the Captain. If the keeper plays well and is efficient he will give the bowler more confidence and also apply pressure to the batsman.

2. Cover-point – Is usually one of the best fielders. First he watches the batsman, his concentration is vital in being aware of the pace of the balls bowled, how the batsman makes his drives and cuts, he must be able to go left or right equally well, often the ball will curve towards his left. Besides taking the hard drive, he has to be aware if the batsman plays shots softly so he can deter the player from taking a quick single.

3. Boundary Fielders – Often have a harder job to concentrate as the ball might not come to them for long periods of time and then only spasmodically, so it is easy to lose concentration. They must remain deep enough for the ball not go over their head, but attack the ball to stop two runs to be scored, they must watch the Captain for positional changes and concentrate in case of catches. Two factors are vital for the Boundary fielder when taking high catches, the first is to gauge where the ball is going to fall before running past it and the other if it is going over you and being able to turn and take it over your shoulder, rather than trying to back peddle.

If you are unable to throw direct to the wicket-keeper from your position, arrange with another fielder that you will throw to him in the form of a relay. This can be quicker than throwing the whole distance yourself. But you must be accurate. Be aware of the slope of the ground, how smooth the outfield is, or if the ball might bounce erratically, all factors require your concentration.

Be aware of where the sun is for yourself and for the fielder or wicket-keeper to whom you are throwing. Similarly, think about the background behind you, as if you have trees there, the receiver might not be able to see the ball. Ensure there is someone backing up if throwing at unguarded stumps. Overthrows not only cost runs but also demoralise the bowler. If you drop a catch, apologise to the bowler and then forget about it, just concentrate harder to catch the next one, everybody drops them sometimes and nobody misses a catch on purpose.

One of the hardest positions to field is short fine leg, unless you attack the ball you are unlikely to be able to stop a run being scored and you need a strong throw, to throw the wicket down at the bowlers' end. Be sure there is someone backing up.

THINK – Concentration For Batsmen

Before you go out to bat you should concentrate on the type of innings you need to make. This will depend on the state of the pitch, whether it is dry, hard and bouncy or if it is cloudy and therefore, likely to swing with the new ball. If they have a good spinner – is it a turning pitch or if the pitch is slower than usual – all these factors should be thought about and you need to concentrate on how you will handle the situation while you are developing your timing. There is a lot of talk about rotation of the strike, often being aware where you may steal a single enables you to keep the score moving without making a strong stroke to endanger losing your wicket.

You need to concentrate on the 'light' as often you might be sitting in the pavilion, but by being outside this is another factor you have covered so as not to misjudge the flight of the ball through suddenly being in strong light.

Practise at concentration, starting with short spells and building the period of concentration.

Times to concentrate specially are:

- When a new bowler starts his spell
- When you start your innings
- Just after a stoppage for drinks
- Prior to the lunch or tea interval or immediately after any break

If you have reached your fifty or hundred, your reaction is to over relax, make a mental note to prepare yourself and concentrate even harder When approaching the batting crease for the first time, do not give any indications to the bowler before you start your innings what your favourite shot is, e.g. many batsmen on the way to the crease will practise their favourite shot. The next time you go out to bat think about this factor.

THINK – Concentration For Bowlers

As the most important factors for all bowlers are LINE and LENGTH, every bowler has to concentrate their mind to decide these two factors both before and during delivery. Precision and accuracy are vital and it takes many hours of practice to ensure that one achieves success some of the time. Once you can change the factors at will, then the next step is to develop the ability to vary the speed of each ball or just some of the balls bowled, if this can be done without giving the batsman any warning that is even better. If you are a slow bowler there are the added factors of varying the trajectory, especially those above the batsman's eye line. All variations require a great deal of patience, persistence, practice and concentration.

If you are a fast bowler, the use of short pitched deliveries, properly directed, are another means of unsettling the batsman.

Each bowler needs to have mastered the technique of using these factors before playing in a match, this will depend on his skills and how well they want to perform.

As discussed in other chapters the need to be able to read the batsman is vital, together with testing out how good the batsman is to resisting your challenge.

Each and every approach is only possible by concentrating and having concentration on these factors.

THINK – Experience

Wherever people of any age test themselves mentally or physically in theory or practice, they all need confidence to do well. Cricket is no different, in fact, confidence plays a huge part in playing cricket well.

Therefore how do we build confidence? Often it is our team-mates who play a large role in our own development of this vital commodity. Memory of past success is probably the greatest item in preparing us for this single process.

THINK – Discipline

Discipline affects everybody; it is part of our daily life from the time we awake in the morning till the time we go to bed at night. Everybody playing or in the administration of cricket is subject to both their own and other players' disciplines.

In cricket we should play within the Laws, playing as correctly as we know how in the recognised interpretation as laid down by the Marylebone Cricket Club, who are custodian of the Laws for The International Cricket Council.

On a personal basis 'Discipline' could be interpreted as pride in one's own ability to perform well. To be fit as possible, to learn the techniques of our own style, whether we are a batsman, bowler or all-rounder. To encourage and support our team-mates and also support our Captain.

Every area of activity is sometimes described as a 'discipline', the definitive description of a particular part of the game. This includes being properly clothed and as smart as possible, because cricketers who appear smarter give the appearance they are better organised and prepared rather than scruffy or untidy teams.

THINK – Psychology

To many the word alone is stress related, and who wants further stress and mental pressure whilst playing their recreational sport? However, if you want to participate in a sport where winning and losing are integral factors of that sport, the success gained from winning and the distress felt by losing create their own pressures. By recognising stress and mental pressure one can use psychology to firstly, reduce them, and secondly, convert them into generating adrenaline. When this is achieved it is like a tonic, mentally building a platform from which further success can be launched – all sports people enjoy success, which, in turn leads to pleasure.

We want to create success in our cricket, and studying mental processes and motives between individuals and within the squad can result in team harmony, which is to everyone's benefit.

Of course organisation, practice and ability are necessary, but eliminating stress and anxiety in favour of a more single-minded approach will make the game less complicated.

The responsibility of offering this approach needs someone with judgement and sensitivity. The person might need experience to deliver an easily acceptable and uncomplicated programme. For the sake of this book we feel that clubs should consider the subject, and are suggesting a minimum basic plan. If a more specific structure is required, then professional advice should be sought.

The use of psychology when talking to a young man who has just been promoted to play for the first eleven, might follow this line:

'Welcome, congratulations on your promotion. Now you are one of this team, we have a slightly different approach to that of the second eleven. We all work for each other; we note and tell each other if errors are creeping into our play. We discuss the fielding positions and where we like to field. We try and remember the good shots we played in an innings and how we may increase these in future innings'.

After the match we tell certain team members that we thought they played well, and what a good performance it was. Alternatively, when discussing how the opposition fared, we talk about their faults and mistakes.

Mental motivation must be developed during training and in practice prior to the match. It helps to set achievable targets in all the main disciplines and it is vital to ensure the team achieves them. Always reward achievement with praise, thus encouraging further improvement next time.

On the field the Captain should never publicly criticise his fellow players and never let them criticise each other, especially if a chance is missed. The best advice is to forget it as quickly as possible. The Captain has the added responsibility of not portraying his negative feelings through body language. For the bowler particularly it is hard to ignore the disappointment when a chance is missed. The bowler must toughen his mental approach and strive to create another batting error by drawing on the motivation developed by the whole team.

THINK – Umpiring And Scoring

Umpiring

Cricket, like no other game, does not have any rules, it has Laws.

This is a fundamental factor for it is how the Laws are interpreted that shapes the way the game is played.

Before any game starts two umpires are appointed. These are then recognised by both captains as the authority for their match.

Unless umpires are appointed you cannot have a cricket match.

It is much better to have two umpires who are not players as then they can concentrate on their umpiring and they can also be impartial.

Each Captain is responsible for the behaviour of his team.

To fully enjoy cricket as a game it helps to know the Laws.

Prior to each game it is the umpires' duty to establish where the boundary is and if there are any local discrepancies such as overhanging branches.

They must know the type of match being played, the timing of intervals and when play finishes. They must synchronise their watches and if there are official scorers make sure their times coincide.

Each umpire should know all the signals he has to use to signal to the scorer what is taking place on the field of play.

(See types of signals displayed as drawings and in written form)

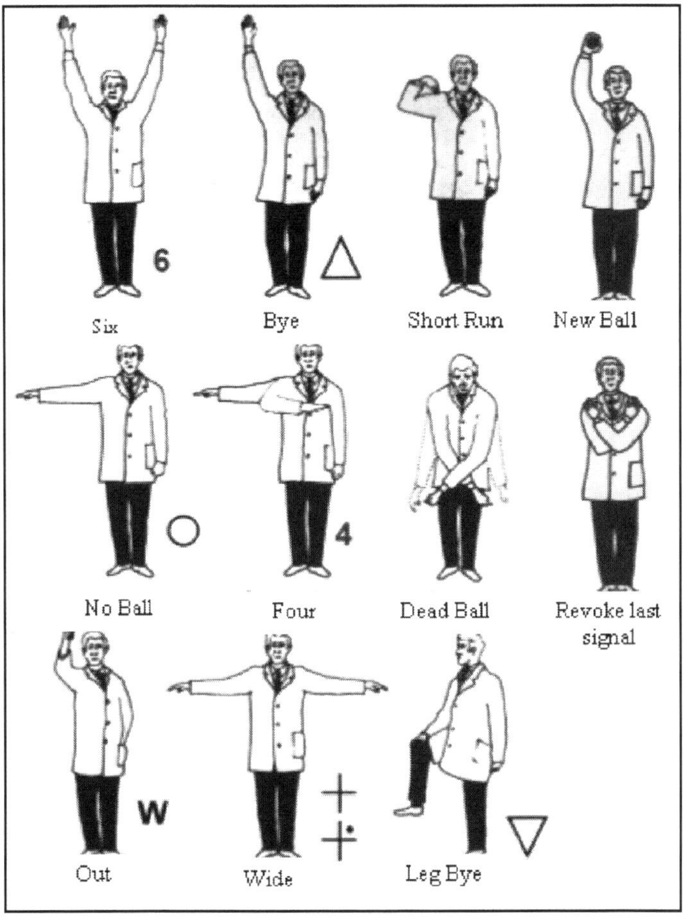

The most important factors for batsmen are the various ways they may be dismissed, which are as follows:

- Bowled
- Caught
- Stumped
- Run Out
- LBW
- Hit wicket
- Hit the ball twice
- Handled the ball
- Obstructing the fielding side
- Timed out

The Law that is questioned most is LBW, this method of being given out should be known by all cricketers, few seem to study it.

It is equally important for bowlers and batsmen to understand this law, as then bowlers will not waste the umpire's time or patience appealing, and batsmen are less likely to infringe the law.

In some forms of cricket a degree of 'sledging' takes place, nobody objects to friendly banter, but bad language and aggressive behaviour has no part to play with real cricket. If directed at you, just smile and realise your opponent is virtually admitting he/she cannot dismiss you by legitimate methods and this is their last hope that you succumb to verbal threats. It will not be long before the tirade dissolves. For it is only if your concentration is broken or you join in that they find sledging works; only in those cases will they continue.

Now the MCC (the arbiter of cricket laws) has produced and encourages a code of behaviour called the 'Spirit of cricket'.

All umpires have to concentrate for long periods for each decision they take is likely to favour one side or the other, making it vital their judgement is correct. If it is proved later that they made the wrong decision remember, errors occur, we all make mistakes, and sometimes so does the umpire. As long as it is an honest one, then all the players should accept it. By the end of the season you will usually find things are balanced out. If the players try and play their best within the laws they will be helping the umpire. In my club we make it an unwritten Law that if we hit the ball and are caught, we do not wait for the umpire – we wait for the appeal and then 'WALK'.

For those who Captain their club or a team, they have a greater responsibility to the umpire, to their team and to the opposition. For the Captain sets the standard, his attitude will be the guide for the other players, even 'body language' is important. If the team has players who are nineteen or younger, the Captain will be expected to prepare for the umpire a list of players and their ages and sign it for the umpire prior to the game commencing. These younger players have strict rules governing where they field, when and when not to wear a helmet, how many overs they are allowed to bowl in a spell, what is the interval between when they bowled last and bowling a new spell. These rules are mandatory.

If you want to cheat, please choose to play a different sport, for nobody likes playing with others who cannot play honestly.

Scoring

All club cricketers should learn how to score, for there are **always** some matches where there is not an official scorer or the one expected fails to turn up.

(See diagrams of all marks made by a scorer displaying the umpire's information from the middle).

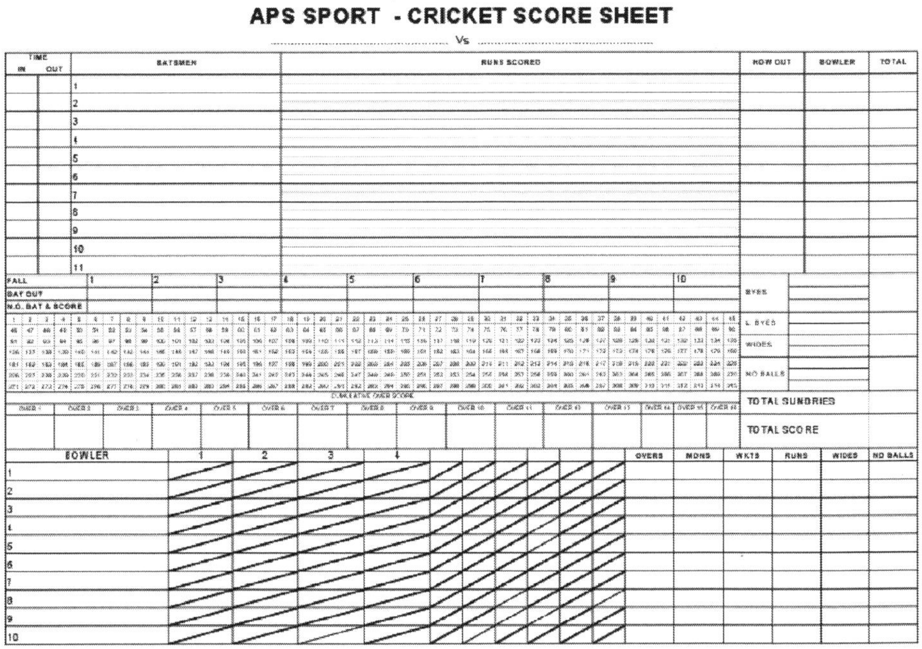

A 15-Minute Guide To Scoring For Players

No cricket match may take place without scorers. The purpose of this Guide is to give players who score for a few overs during a game the confidence to take their turn as a scorer to ensure that a match can take place.

The Batting Section Of The Scoring Record

- You should have received a team list, hopefully with the batting order identified.
- Record the name of the batsman in pencil or as the innings progresses - captains often change the batting order!
- Indicate the captain with an asterisk (*) and the wicket-keeper with a dagger symbol (†).
- When a batsman is out, draw diagonal lines // in the 'Runs Scored' section after all entries for that batsman to show that the innings is completed.
- Record the method of dismissal in the "how out" column.
- Write the bowler's name in the "bowler" column only if the bowler gets credit for the dismissal.
- When a batsman's innings is completed record his total score.

Cumulative Score

- Use one stroke to cross off each incident of runs scored.
- When more than one run is scored and the total is taken onto the next row of the cumulator this should be indicated as shown below.

  Cumulative Run Tally

  1 2 3 4 5 6 7 8 9

  10 1 2 3 4 5 7 7 8 9

End Of Over Score

- At the end of each over enter the total score, number of wickets fallen and bowler number.

The Bowling Section Of The Scoring Record

The Over

- Always record the balls in the over in the same sequence in the overs' box.
- An over containing Wide or No balls, show balls 7 & 8 as highlighted.
  1 2 3 1 3 5 1 7 2 1 7 4
  7 8 7 8 3 8 4 2 8 5
  4 5 6 2 4 6 5 6 3 6
- All balls bowled must be entered.
- If the umpire gives a 7 ball over record a 7 ball over.
- If there are only 5 deliveries in the over that is all you should record.
- A Maiden over is a complete over by a single bowler in which there is no score against that bowler. The dots should be joined together to form an "M".
- A Maiden over cannot contain a Wide ball or a No ball.
- An accidental 5 or 7 ball over is a completed over when counting up the number of overs bowled. As a completed over, it can be a Maiden over.
- A part over for any other reason can never be a Maiden over.
- If a wicket falls that is credited to the bowler enter a "w" for that delivery.
- If a wicket credited to the bowler falls in a Maiden over it becomes a 'wicket maiden'. Join dots and "w" together to form a "W".
- Numerals are used only for runs made when the ball has been struck by the bat.

Byes And Leg Byes

- Can be entered as a dot but it is better to use a symbol. Byes B or Triangle, point upwards. Leg byes L or Triangle, point down.
- Runs made as byes or leg byes are recorded in the appropriate line of fielding extras.

Wides And No Balls

- Under MCC Laws of Cricket a one-run penalty is awarded for a No ball or a Wide in addition to any other runs made.
- All Wide balls and No balls count against the bowler in the bowling analysis.
- An over containing a Wide ball or a No ball cannot be a maiden over.
- A Wide or a No ball is not a fair delivery and does not count as a ball in the over.
- If a wicket falls when a Wide ball or No ball has been bowled and there are no other runs, record the one-run penalty before entering the score at the fall of the wicket.

Summarise The Bowling

- Complete the total number of overs, maidens, runs and wickets for each bowler at the end of the innings.
- If an over is incomplete each fair delivery in the part over is expressed as 0.1 ball.
- Calculate and record the number of no ball and wide deliveries, the total number of balls bowled and the average for each bowler.
- Total these figures to provide a summary of balls, overs, maidens, runs and wickets for the entire innings.

A match cannot take place if there is not a scorer.The scorer must be able to have a clear view of the cricket ground, whilst the game is in play.

Each team Captain should advise the scorer as follows:

The team's batting order, who their bowlers are likely to be and the name of the wicket-keeper.

The scorer will need to know what type of game is to be played, when the intervals are and the start time and finish.

The scorer should be told who wins the toss.

If there are two scorers then they should ensure they agree the score at the end of each over, when a wicket falls and at any breaks in play. The more information they can put into the scoresheet, the better it will be for the players and anybody reporting the game. Their neatness and tidiness in completing the scorebook is very important. Both teams should have an accurate report of the match.

Information can be gained from your County Cricket Board or County Cricket Development Officer on how to find out where training courses are being held.

If you wish to become either an umpire or scorer, you will have to register with the CRB. This is mandatory, both as a safeguard for the players and for yourself. It will help you if you join the new body; many of the courses and updated information will be cheaper if gained through the County Boards.

There is also a very helpful website: **www.acumenbooks.co.uk**
Telephone number: **+44 (0) 1782 720753**
Fax Number: **+44 (0) 1782 720 798**
Or **www.lords.org**

Acknowledgements

When writing a book there is an urgency for all component parts to come together with the least delay, therefore the authors would like to express their wholehearted appreciation to everyone who has contributed to this task, because besides the contribution there was always an immediate deadline. Jocelyn Galsworthy provided inspiration as well as her very special artistry with many of the cartoons, successfully interpreting our sketches.

They are enormously grateful to John Barclay for writing his Foreword, to Christopher Laine for contributions to the chapter on wicket-keeping and to Graham Fielding for his cartoons.

They would like to thank the Rodin Museum in Paris for graciously permitting the reproduction of 'The Thinker'. They were indebted to the late David Money, successful author and cricketer, for his contributions to the subject matter and manuscript presentation.

They would like to thank Peter Came, Rupert Cox and John Barclay for their expert guidance with some of the updating for the second edition.

They greatly appreciate the efforts made by Michael Massey to promote and generate sales for this book.

Finally they wish to thank Cliff Booth, Colin Pearson, Fraser Stewart, and Rob White and their many cricketing friends who gave their encouragement and shared their experiences with enthusiasm.

THE CRICKETERS' WHO'S WHO 2011

A totally revamped title with a thought-provoking foreword from Alastair Cook, Cricketers Who's Who is in its 32nd year and has finally grown up! A dramatically enhanced county-by-county guide to the game, with focus on the major stars, the players to watch and this year's tourists, Sri Lanka and India.

Out this April – RRP £19.99

ISBN 978-1-907803-53-6

ALSO AVAILABLE

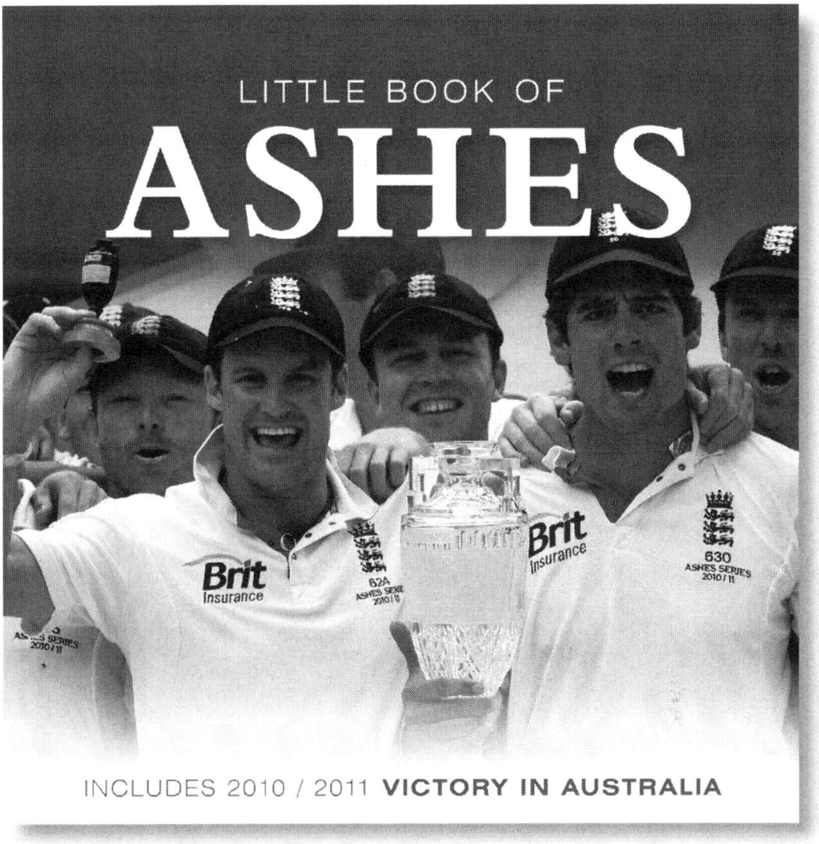